IRAN NUCLEAR NEGOTIATIONS AFTER THE SECOND EXTENSION: WHERE ARE THEY GOING?

HEARING

BEFORE THE

COMMITTEE ON FOREIGN AFFAIRS
HOUSE OF REPRESENTATIVES

ONE HUNDRED FOURTEENTH CONGRESS

FIRST SESSION

JANUARY 27, 2015

Serial No. 114–5

Printed for the use of the Committee on Foreign Affairs

Available via the World Wide Web: http://www.foreignaffairs.house.gov/ or http://www.gpo.gov/fdsys/

U.S. GOVERNMENT PUBLISHING OFFICE

92–850PDF   WASHINGTON : 2015

For sale by the Superintendent of Documents, U.S. Government Publishing Office
Internet: bookstore.gpo.gov   Phone: toll free (866) 512–1800; DC area (202) 512–1800
Fax: (202) 512–2104   Mail: Stop IDCC, Washington, DC 20402–0001

COMMITTEE ON FOREIGN AFFAIRS

EDWARD R. ROYCE, California, *Chairman*

CHRISTOPHER H. SMITH, New Jersey
ILEANA ROS-LEHTINEN, Florida
DANA ROHRABACHER, California
STEVE CHABOT, Ohio
JOE WILSON, South Carolina
MICHAEL T. McCAUL, Texas
TED POE, Texas
MATT SALMON, Arizona
DARRELL E. ISSA, California
TOM MARINO, Pennsylvania
JEFF DUNCAN, South Carolina
MO BROOKS, Alabama
PAUL COOK, California
RANDY K. WEBER SR., Texas
SCOTT PERRY, Pennsylvania
RON DeSANTIS, Florida
MARK MEADOWS, North Carolina
TED S. YOHO, Florida
CURT CLAWSON, Florida
SCOTT DesJARLAIS, Tennessee
REID J. RIBBLE, Wisconsin
DAVID A. TROTT, Michigan
LEE M. ZELDIN, New York
TOM EMMER, Minnesota

ELIOT L. ENGEL, New York
BRAD SHERMAN, California
GREGORY W. MEEKS, New York
ALBIO SIRES, New Jersey
GERALD E. CONNOLLY, Virginia
THEODORE E. DEUTCH, Florida
BRIAN HIGGINS, New York
KAREN BASS, California
WILLIAM KEATING, Massachusetts
DAVID CICILLINE, Rhode Island
ALAN GRAYSON, Florida
AMI BERA, California
ALAN S. LOWENTHAL, California
GRACE MENG, New York
LOIS FRANKEL, Florida
TULSI GABBARD, Hawaii
JOAQUIN CASTRO, Texas
ROBIN L. KELLY, Illinois
BRENDAN F. BOYLE, Pennsylvania

AMY PORTER, *Chief of Staff*   THOMAS SHEEHY, *Staff Director*

JASON STEINBAUM, *Democratic Staff Director*

CONTENTS

IRAN NUCLEAR NEGOTIATIONS AFTER THE SECOND EXTENSION: WHERE ARE THEY GOING?

TUESDAY, JANUARY 27, 2015

House of Representatives,
Committee on Foreign Affairs,
Washington, DC.

The committee met, pursuant to notice, at 10:07 a.m., in room 2172 Rayburn House Office Building, Hon. Edward Royce (chairman of the committee) presiding.

Chairman ROYCE. I will ask all the members if you could take your seats and this hearing will come to order.

This morning we are looking at the prospects for reaching a viable nuclear agreement with Iran; one that increases our national security. This has been, and will continue to be one of the committee's top priorities. For those of us that have worked on his issue for a number of years like Ileana Ros-Lehtinen and myself, Mr. Sherman, Mr. Engel, we remember well last year or last session. We presented legislation here that I and Mr. Engel authored that passed this committee unanimously that attempted to bring more pressure on Iran by giving the Ayatollah a choice between economic collapse or compromise on his nuclear weapons program. It passed here unanimously, as I mentioned, and in the floor of the House of Representatives, 400 to 20.

Some would argue—certainly we believe this—that the leverage that we brought to bear has helped bring Iran to the table. But we have dealt with administrations in the past, whether Democrat or Republican. Mr. Sherman and I can tell you in terms of sitting through many of these meetings, our frustrations with the delay in really bringing the type of leverage and sanctions to bear on Iran to get the type of deal that we thought was verifiable.

Now we have had a decade now of diplomatic negotiations over Iran's pursuit of nuclear technology in violation of the U.N. Security Council Resolutions on this subject. These have reached their height over the past year, as the Obama administration, along with the UK, France, Russia, China, and Germany, have been seeking to negotiate a ''long-term comprehensive solution'' to Iran's illicit nuclear program. During these talks, Iran has agreed to limit its nuclear program temporarily in return for some sanctions relief.

A final agreement would free Iran of sanctions, which was, by the way, in our view at least, driven to the negotiating table by the previous sanctions that we had enacted here, while allowing it to maintain a ''mutually defined enrichment program,'' to be treated like any other ''non-nuclear weapon state party to the Nonprolifera-tion Treaty.'' That best case would leave Iran as a threshold nu-clear state. But worse, any limits placed on Iran's nuclear program as part of the ''comprehensive solution'' would, of course, based on this agreement, expire. Maybe in 10 years, maybe sooner. But there is an expiration that is being discussed right now in the agreement.

Negotiations, now into their second extension, appear to be stale-mated. That is even after U.S. negotiators move closer and closer to Iranian positions. According to the administration, ''big gaps'' re-main, and a senior official hinted last week that talks may extend again come June's deadline.

Meanwhile, the Ayatollah, since he is the one that makes the final decision here, has been advancing Iranian nuclear programs: Pursuing new reactors; testing a new generation of centrifuges, and operating Iran's illicit procurement network. These actions clearly violate the spirit of the interim agreement. Yet, the administration appears more concerned that sanctions, designed to strengthen its negotiating hand, and which would have no impact, no impact, un-less Iran walks away from negotiations, could sink an agreement. So let us be clear. If an agreement is sunk, it is because Iran has no interest in abandoning its drive to nuclear weapons, which is what many of us believe.

Of course, Iran's nuclear work isn't Iran's only provocation. While Iranian diplomats put on a good face in a European negotiating room, its IRGC, its Quds Forces, and other proxies have been busy working to influence and ultimately dominate the region. And this is what we hear from the Gulf States and from our other allies throughout the region. Iran is boosting Assad in Syria and Hezbollah continues to threaten Israel. In '06, I watched as those rockets from Iran and Syria came down on Haifa. Today, there are 100,000 such rockets, thanks to Iran's production. And Iranian-sup-plied rockets to Hamas rained down recently on Israel. Frankly, last week, an Iranian-backed militia displaced the government in Yemen, something that we had heard about from the Ambassadors from throughout that region; their concern that the Iranians were going to topple that government. It was, frankly, the toppling of a key counterterrorism partner of ours. Most in the region see Iran pocketing a nuclear deal and continuing with its domination, cer-tainly no winning game plan to stabilize the Middle East. Not to mention that Iran's horrendous repression at home continues. This isn't a negotiating partner that gives much confidence.

If we are going to have any chance of a deal that advances U.S. national security interests, Iran's leaders have to feel that their only choice is a verifiable and meaningful agreement. We are far from it. Worse, many in the region feel Iran is on the rise. Falling oil prices should strengthen our hand, but the Obama administra-tion has yet to explain a single change as to how it will negotiate differently with Iran over the coming months, it raises questions. And while the administration reaches for a deal, it should do so un-derstanding the regime's duplicity and militancy. And when I say its militancy, the fact that the Ayatollah still leads chants of ''Death to America'' and ''Death to Israel'' and Iran still speaks of Israel as ''the one bomb country'' and still speaks of its long-term confrontation with the U.S., this again gives the members pause who have dealt with Iran for a long period of time.

In addition to more economic pressure, we should have an Iran policy with thought-provoking broadcasting to inspire Iranian dissent, a focus on its horrendous human rights abuses and illicit procurement networks, as well as bolstering allies in the region that face Iranian aggression.

As one former intelligence official told the committee last year, "Iran's nuclear program is just the tip of a revolutionary spear that extends across the world and threatens key U.S. interests." This is a regime that is playing for keeps. Yet sometimes it seems the administration is more concerned about Congress moving on sanctions than pressuring its treacherous and deadly negotiating partner that is on the other side of that table.

We look forward to hearing from our witnesses today on the future of these discussions and options we can pursue that would truly end the threat of a nuclear-armed Iran. And I will now turn to Mr. Brad Sherman of California for his remarks.

Mr. SHERMAN. Thank you, Mr. Chairman, for holding these critical hearings, our ranking member, Eliot Engel, has been asked by the President to join the administration in the memorial service for King Abdullah of Saudi Arabia.

Some may ask why we are having these hearings at all here in Congress. After all, the Executive Branch may take the position that Congress is only an advisory body when it comes to foreign affairs. I think we have a co-decisionmaking responsibility and that is why I think we need our witnesses here to guide us in making those decisions.

We have universal agreement on the goal: Prevent Iran from having nuclear weapons. But we need to get down to the fine points. What will a good agreement look like? What sanctions should we impose if Iran does not agree to a good deal by June 30th? And who, or what body here in Washington will be answering these questions? Is it Congress' role only to advise the President? Or are we supposed to pass laws that are carried out?

Now Iran is operating under the twice extended Joint Action Plan. It is inaccurate, as some have said, to say that that plan has halted their program. The centrifuges continue to turn. They build their stockpile of 3½ percent enriched uranium. It may be oxidized, but it can be returned to gaseous form, ready for further enrichment rather easily. And of course, this analysis doesn't even include their work on more powerful gas centrifuges, their weaponization program, etcetera.

But the Joint Action Plan has impeded the Iranian program and it is better than nothing. Their 20 percent enriched uranium has been diluted in most cases or to a great degree. So Iran is a little further away from their first bomb or at least having highly-enriched uranium for it, but is getting closer every day to their sixth, seventh, or eighth bomb as they continue to build an increasingly large stockpile of low-enriched uranium. And it is counter intuitive, but as I think our witnesses will illustrate, going from uranium ore to 3½ percent enriched uranium, even 3½ percent enriched uranium oxide is more than half the work. Going from 3½ percent to 93 percent, is the easier part of that effort.

So the issue then is whether we should have sanctions that go into effect on July 1. The fact is Iran has a July 1 program. They just haven't had to publish it because they don't have an open society where they have to make decisions in public. We ought to have a July 1 program ready to go and in order to do that, Congress actually has to vote on a bill, rather than not vote until July.

Now a little history, until 2010 our sanctions toward Iran were modest at most, certainly not enough to dissuade them in 2010. The President signs CISADA. We got the Menendez-Kirk sanctions and we finally began to put some reasonable pressure on Iran. Keep in mind the last administration presented us from passing any new meaningful legislation, or at least any new major legislation. And the Obama administration opposed sanctions in its first few years. But the Obama administration has done a commendable job of enforcing the laws that Congress has passed, even the ones we passed over their objections.

We have frozen Iranian assets around the world. We have forced a decline in their oil exports, but they were still estimating 2 percent economic growth. That growth will be lower because of the decline of oil prices, but the Iranian economy is slated to grow far faster than a majority of countries in the EU.

I do want to pick up on the chairman's comments about broadcasting. One approach is that we simply rebroadcast into Iran the many Farsi language programs made in California. Now some are politically incorrect. We shouldn't endorse anything there, but we could get those retransmitted for pennies a minute and let 1,000 or at least a dozen flowers bloom where the Iranian people can hear all of these different views being presented in their own language free from U.S. Government control.

As to evaluating the agreement, I think that in addition to looking at how robust their centrifuge program is, we have to ask how much uranium will Iran be able to retain in its stockpiles. We can do a lot even if they have more centrifuges than we would want if every night the uranium enriched is exported to some other country.

Finally, we could reach a compromise with the administration on the whole issue of the timing of legislation. They have said that they are going to come up with—talking to them last night—a good agreement on the political matters by the end of March. So let us pass a bill in the House. Let us pass a bill in the Senate and let us go to conference. And let us wait to see what the administration can prepare, but only if the administration agrees that they will stop efforts to delay new sanctions at that point, except to show us the non-technical agreement in principle reached in Switzerland. Instead, the President and the administration asks us to slow down for this reason and then later slow down for that reason and then they are free to tell us to slow down for the next reason, only because we acted faster than the administration wanted and we brought Iran to this point. And I yield back.

Chairman ROYCE. I thank the gentleman for yielding. Before we go to our witnesses, I will just mention that I think Mr. Sherman's concept of broadcasting into Iran, also some of these cultural programs because we forget that the Ayatollah has made it a sin or interprets it as a sin for women to sing. So a lot of popular music and programs—I remember when that tune ''Happy'' was recorded by some young women in Iran and boy, did they feel the lash because they had sung to that tune. And I think at times we are not really focused on the nature of just how brutal this regime is on its own people, especially on women, and the way in which a regime treats its own people will sometimes tell you a lot about how they might treat their neighbors.

Let us go to our distinguished group of experts. Ambassador Eric Edelman is a Distinguished Fellow at the Center for Strategic and Budgetary Assessments. Previously, he served as U.S. Ambassador to Finland during the Clinton administration and to Turkey. Ambassador Edelman also served as Under Secretary for Defense Policy from 2005 to 2009.

Mr. John Hannah is a Senior Fellow at the Foundation for Defense of Democracies. He previously served as National Security Advisor to the Vice President from 2005 to 2009. Mr. Hannah has also worked at the State Department.

Dr. Ray Takeyh is a Senior Fellow for Middle East Studies at the Council on Foreign Relations. He previously served as Senior Advisor on Iran at the State Department and was Professor at the National Defense University.

Mr. Einhorn, Robert Einhorn is a Senior Fellow at the Brookings Institution and before joining Brookings in 2013, he served as the State Department's Special Advisor for Non-Proliferation and Arms Control. And he was Senior Advisor at the Center for Strategic and International Studies.

And without objection, the witnesses' full, prepared statementswill be made part of the record. And members will have 5 calendar days to submit statements and questions and extraneous material for the record. So we will start with Ambassador Edelman. If you all would just summarize your remarks to 5 minutes, that would be perfect. Thank you.

STATEMENT OF THE HONORABLE ERIC S. EDELMAN, DISTINGUISHED FELLOW, CENTER FOR STRATEGIC AND BUDGETARY ASSESSMENTS

Mr. EDELMAN. Mr. Chairman, I will do my best. First, I would like to thank you and Ranking Member Engel and Mr. Sherman and the other members of the committee for giving me the opportunity to appear today to discuss the implications of the current negotiations on Iran nuclear matters. I remember well, Mr. Royce, the codel that you led to Turkey when I was Ambassador more than 10 years ago when one of the issues we discussed because, of course, Turkey is one of Iran's neighbors, was this very subject. And what I hope to do today is provide both a little bit of a retrospective look back and also a prospective look forward on where we stand with Iran.

Preventing a nuclear weapons capable Iran remains, I think, the most pressing national security challenge facing the United States today. As President Obama himself said in a speech he gave in 2012, ''a nuclear-armed Iran is not a challenge that can be contained. It would threaten the elimination of Israel, the security of the Gulf nations, and the stability of the global economy. It risks triggering a nuclear arms race in the region and the unraveling of the nonproliferation treaty.''

I would submit that the turmoil we currently see in the region is in no small part a reflection of Iran's ''struggle for mastery'' in the Middle East where its aspirations and involvement in a series of conflicts have created a dynamic that drives both Sunni and Shi'a extremism throughout the area and threatens the regional power balance.

In Iraq, Iran's patronage of Shi'a militias before and especially since the departure of U.S. forces in December 2011 has disrupted the domestic political balance and fed the recrudescence of Sunni Islamist extremism manifested in the resurgence of the Islamic State last year.

In Syria, the IRGC provides the money, oil, weaponry and with the help of Hezbollah, front-line soldiers that the al-Assad regime needs to grind down the moderate Sunni opposition. This, in turn, feeds the radicalization of the Sunni population and provides fertile ground for recruiting by the al Nusra front and the Islamic State. Iranian policy also strains Lebanon's delicate political balance and its Western-backed armed forces, thereby increasing the odds of another round of war between Israel and Lebanon. And as you noted in your opening statement, much of Hamas' arsenal and combat training have come from Iran, including many of the weapons it used to attack Israeli civilians this past summer.

Finally, again, as you noted in your statement, Houthi rebels in Yemen have taken over much of the country in recent weeks, culminating in the resignation of President Hadi and Prime Minister Bahah and the collapse of that fragile country's counterterrorism cooperation with the United States against AQAP. This is a development I want to stress that threatens the homeland security of the homeland as well as that of our European allies.

Iran's regional revisionism is already proceeding at a breath-taking pace even without the sword and shield that a nuclear weapons capability would provide it. It is no wonder that our traditional allies in the region worry that a nuclear armed Iran or even an Iran on the threshold of nuclear weapons would be emboldened to sow even more havoc in the region.

The prospect of Iran crossing the nuclear threshold has spawned more than a decade of diplomacy intended to restrict its potential pathways to a bomb. But unfortunately, in my view, the objectives of these negotiations have become steadily more limited over the years, as Iran's intransigence has led the United States and its diplomatic partners to repeatedly define down their red lines in favor of Iran's.

On the eve of the Joint Plan of Action, with Iran perched on the nuclear threshold, a task force that I co-chair with Dennis Ross, spelled out a series of benchmarks for an acceptable final deal. We argued that any such agreement would have to tangibly roll back Iran's ability to produce enough weapons-grade uranium for a nuclear device, impose a strict inspections regime, adhere to international legal requirements, and resolve the outstanding concerns of the International Atomic Energy Agency. To pressure Iran to meet these standards, the U.S. and its allies would need to negotiate from a position of strength and implement a strict deadline for the talks. And I would add use the leverage that the Congress has provided it.

Unhappily, the comprehensive agreement outlined by the Joint Plan of Action reflects the P5+1's receding red lines. And as such, I think it falls short of the aforementioned principles, to the serious detriment of U.S. national security.

Despite constant assurances from administration officials, including Secretary Kerry that ''a bad deal is worse than no deal,'' the pattern of concessions and the negotiating dynamic that has been established give very strong reasons for outside observers to feel that that the negotiations are moving far beyond the parameters of an acceptable final agreement.

It is difficult to envisage such an agreement without a change in the trajectory of these negotiations, and without a decisive change in Iran's calculus of its own best interests. American policymakers must use all available instruments of coercive diplomacy to restore credibility to the oft-repeated statement that every option remains on the table to prevent a nuclear Iran. Success is only possible if Iran realizes it has more to lose from the failure of diplomacy.

The U.S. retains an ability to exert pressure through sanctions. Moreover, I would argue that today given the current oil market, the balance is highly disadvantageous to Iran. Not to put too fine a point on it, given the current price of oil, we don't need to fear that having Iranian oil off the market would roil international markets and set back the recovery of the global economy. For these reasons, the United States can credibly threaten more stringent measures against energy and other vital sectors if Iran continues its obstinacy.

I think American policymakers should clarify and strengthen our declaratory policy. I think it would be useful for the Congress to hold hearings on the feasibility of the military option in publicizing some of the advanced U.S. military capabilities, such as the GBU–57 Massive Ordnance Penetrator, a bunker buster designed specifically to reach targets like Iran's deeply-buried illegal nuclear facilities.

The United States should also boost the credibility of Israel's military option as well.

Finally, as one of the other panelists and I argued recently in the press, the United States must be willing to compete with Iran rather than actively seeking its partnership. On one level, this requires a change in tone, but the administration must emphasize its readiness to exert more pressure on Iran instead of exerting pressure on Congress with talking points that come to quote a ranking member of the Senate, ''straight out of Tehran.''

Mr. Chairman, I thank you again and your colleagues for scheduling this hearing and the members for their patience and consideration and I look forward to the rest of the hearing and answering any questions.

[The prepared statement of Mr. Edelman follows:]

Statement of the Hon. Eric Edelman
Distinguished Fellow, Center for Strategic and Budgetary Assessments
Co-Chair, Iran Task Force at JINSA Gemunder Center

"Iran Nuclear Negotiations After the Second Extension:
Where Are They Going?"
Committee on Foreign Affairs
U.S. House of Representatives
January 27, 2015

Mr. Chairman, Ranking Member Engel, Members of the Committee, thank you for giving me the opportunity to appear before you today to discuss the implications of the Obama Administration's approach to the Iran nuclear negotiations. I have followed this issue for more than a decade, first as the U.S. Ambassador to Turkey and then as Under Secretary of Defense for Policy. Since retiring from government service in 2009 I have continued to track the progress of Iran's nuclear program and worked with several of my colleagues at the Center for Strategic and Budgetary Assessments on the broader threat that the program presents to the nuclear non-proliferation regime and regional security in the Middle East. I am also the co-chair with Ambassador Dennis Ross of a bipartisan Iran Task Force sponsored by JINSA's Gemunder Center for Defense and Strategy that has produced a series of detailed appraisals of the negotiations. Today I will try to provide a strategic assessment of where we stand in the ongoing nuclear negotiations with Iran.[1]

The Iranian Strategic Threat

---

[1] Eric S. Edelman, Andrew F. Krepinevich, Evan B. Montgomery, "The Dangers of a Nuclear Iran: The Limits of Containment," *Foreign Affairs*, 90:1, pps. 66-81; and Krepinevich, *Critical Mass: Nuclear Proliferation in the Middle East*, (Washington, DC: CSBA, 2013): the reports issued by the Gemunder Center's Iran Task Force can be found at: www.jinsa.org/gemunder-center-iran-task-force

Preventing a nuclear weapons-capable Iran remains the most pressing national security challenge facing the United States today. As President Obama said in his U.N. General Assembly speech in 2012, "a nuclear-armed Iran is not a challenge that can be contained. It would threaten the elimination of Israel, the security of Gulf nations, and the stability of the global economy. It risks triggering a nuclear-arms race in the region and the unraveling of the non-proliferation treaty."[2]

Even without a nuclear weapons capability, Iranian policies underscore this assessment and reflect Tehran's ambition to displace the United States and exert its hegemony as the dominant regional power. The turmoil we currently see in the region is in no small part a reflection of Iran's "struggle for mastery" in the Middle East where it's aspirations and involvement in a series of conflicts have created a dynamic that drives both Sunni and Shi'a extremism throughout the area and threatens the regional power balance.[3]

In Iraq, Iran's patronage of Shi'a militias before and especially since the departure of U.S. forces in December 2011 has disrupted the domestic political balance among ethnic and sectarian groups and fed the recrudescence of Sunni Islamist extremism manifested in the resurgence of the Islamic State last year. The United States' goal of a pluralistic, unitary state to ultimately defeat the Islamic State is currently threatened by Iran's overt political and military intervention on behalf of radical Shiite militias.

---

[2] White House Office of the Press Secretary, "Remarks by the President to the UN General Assembly," September 25, 2012.

[3] The English historian AJP Taylor coined the term "struggle for mastery" to describe the European state system as it sought to maintain a balance of power while coping with the rise of Germany, see Taylor, *The Struggle for Mastery in Europe: 1848-1918* (Oxford: Oxford University Press, 1954). The struggle over the regional balance of power in the Middle East has also been examined in Efraim Karsh and Inari Karsh, *Empires of the Sand: The Struggle for Mastery in the Middle East, 1789-1923,* (Cambridge, MA: Harvard University Press, 1999) it has also been applied to the contemporary rise of China in the East Asia, see Aaron L. Friedberg, *A Contest for Supremacy: China, America, and the Struggle for Mastery in Asia* (New York: W.W. Norton, 2011).

The fact that senior Iranian Revolutionary Guards officers are being killed in Iraq attests to the brazenness and depth of Iranian involvement.

In Syria, Iran's hardline Islamic Revolutionary Guard Corps (IRGC) provides the money, oil, weaponry and – with the help of Hezbollah – front-line soldiers that the al-Assad regime needs to grind down the moderate Sunni opposition. This, in turn, feeds the radicalization of the Sunni population and provides fertile ground for recruiting by both the al Nusra front and the Islamic State. By involving Hezbollah so deeply in this sectarian civil war, Iranian policy also strains Lebanon's delicate political balance and its Western-backed armed forces thereby increasing the odds of another round of war between Israel and Lebanon. Much of Hamas's arsenal and combat training have come from Iran, including many of the weapons it used to attack Israeli civilians and troops this past summer. According to the U.S. State Department, the IRGC has also attempted to ship arms to opposition groups in Bahrain, home to the U.S. Fifth Fleet.[4]

Finally, Iranian-backed Houthi rebels in Yemen have taken over much of the country in recent months culminating in the resignation of President Abu Rabbu Mansour Hadi and Prime Minister Khaled Bahah and the collapse of that fragile country's counterterrorism cooperation with the United States against al-Qaeda in the Arabian Peninsula (AQAP). This development threatens the homeland security of the United States and our European allies.

---

[4] U.S. Department of State, Bureau of Counterterrorism, "Country Reports on Terrorism 2013: State Sponsors of Terrorism Overview," April 2014. The recent Israeli strike that killed a senior IRGC officer in the company of second generation terror master Jihad Mughniyah again testifies to Iran's hand in stirring up additional violence and conflict in the region.

It also gives Iran leverage against Saudi Arabia, and raises the risk to shipping along the Bab el-Mandeb Strait, which the Energy Information Administration calls a "world oil transit chokepoint critical to global energy security."[5]

Iran's regional revisionism is already proceeding at a breath taking pace even without the sword and shield that a nuclear weapons capability would provide. It is no wonder that our traditional allies in the region worry that a nuclear armed Iran or even an Iran on the nuclear threshold would be emboldened to sow even more havoc in the region.[6]

Receding Diplomatic Redlines

Given Iran's behavior without a nuclear weapons capability, and bearing in mind the threat to the global nuclear non-proliferation regime, the prospect of Iran crossing this threshold has spawned more than a decade of diplomacy intended to restrict its potential pathways to a bomb. Unfortunately, the objectives of these negotiations have become steadily more limited over the years, as Iranian intransigence has led the United States and its diplomatic partners to repeatedly define down their redlines in favor of Tehran's. Starting in 2003-6, the EU-3 (Britain, France and Germany), followed by the P5+1 (the EU-3 joined by China, Russia and the United States) and the U.N. Security Council, demanded that Iran verifiably suspend uranium enrichment and reprocessing.[7] Though Iran cooperated at first, it eventually resumed these activities in 2005 and began expanding its nuclear program the following year.

---

[5] U.S. Energy Information Administration, "World Oil Transit Chokepoints," November 10, 2014.
[6] For an excellent recent survey of Iran's bold moves see Charles Krauthammer, "Iran's Emerging Empire," *Washington Post*, January 22, 2015.
[7] U.N. Security Council Resolution 1696 (July 31, 2006) demanded Iran suspend its uranium enrichment, a demand that was reaffirmed in subsequent UNSCRs in 2007, 2008 and 2010.

By 2009, the P5+1 no longer insisted that Iran halt enrichment, but only that it ship out much of its 5% low-enriched uranium (LEU) stockpile for conversion to medical research reactor fuel. Iran rejected such offers on the grounds they did not recognize its declared "right" to enrich, and started enriching 20% LEU at its previously-clandestine Fordow facility. In mid-2012, the P5+1's desiderata were whittled down to "stop, shut, ship:" stop 20% LEU enrichment, shut Fordow and ship out the 20% LEU stockpile – in the process abandoning their demand that Iran ship out any of its 5% LEU stockpile. Less than a year later, as Iran's nuclear program continued to grow, the P5+1 also dropped its insistence that Iran shutter Fordow. Thus the Joint Plan of Action (JPA), which was agreed later that year, allowed Fordow to remain open, and though Iran agreed to suspend 20% LEU enrichment, it would not ship out any stockpiles.

Implications for a Final Deal

On the eve of the JPA, with Iran perched on the nuclear threshold, our Task Force issued a report spelling out the benchmarks for an acceptable final deal.[8] Any such agreement would have to tangibly roll back Iran's ability to produce enough weapons-grade uranium for a nuclear device, impose a strict inspections regime, adhere to international legal requirements, and resolve outstanding concerns of the International Atomic Energy Agency (IAEA). To pressure Iran to meet these standards, the United States and its allies would need to negotiate from a position of strength and implement a strict deadline for the talks.

---

[8] JINSA's Gemunder Center Iran Task Force, "Principles for Diplomacy with Iran," October 14, 2013: http://www.jinsa.org/publications/principles-diplomacy-iran

Unhappily, the comprehensive agreement outlined by the JPA reflects the P5+1's receding redlines. As such, they fall far short of the aforementioned principles, to the serious detriment of U.S. national security. Under the comprehensive agreement foreseen in the JPA, Iran would retain enough key aspects of its enrichment program to continue progress toward nuclear weapons capability, including its facilities and LEU stockpiles, despite remaining in violation of five legally binding U.N. Security Council resolutions calling on it to suspend enrichment and reprocessing. Though it agreed to broader IAEA inspections under a final deal, its enrichment program, even with the increased monitoring under the Additional Protocol, would be far from transparent. Moreover, all existing U.S., E.U. and U.N. sanctions would be lifted. Even these restrictions would not be permanent: after the deal's sunset, Iran would possess a normalized, industrial-sized nuclear program.

Equally worrisome, the agreement does not appear to be contingent on addressing the other two components of nuclear capability beyond fissile material: a nuclear warhead and a delivery vehicle. Iran is working separately with the IAEA on concerns over possible military dimensions (PMD) of its nuclear program, including weaponization research. It is also entirely unclear if delivery vehicles are part of the discussion, despite Iran continuing its work on advancing the largest ballistic missile arsenal in the Middle East.

Heading for a Bad Deal

Despite constant assurances from Administration officials, including Secretary Kerry that "a bad deal is worse than no deal," the pattern of concessions and negotiating dynamic outlined above give very strong reasons for outside observes to fear that the negotiations are moving far beyond the parameters of an acceptable final agreement.[9] Although it is not possible to offer a judgment at this point, because the Administration has said, "nothing is agreed until everything is agreed," it still appears likely that we may be confronted with a very bad deal sometime soon. The Administration has retreated from a succession of redlines on uranium enrichment, to the point where Iran could be allowed to retain the majority of its existing enrichment infrastructure. Many of the reported proposals being floated by the U.S. negotiators, whether they would disconnect parts of installed centrifuges, cap Iran's centrifuge levels or limit its total enrichment output, would still leave Iran with a latent nuclear weapons capability that it could expand and upgrade without violating a final deal.

Even then, giving ground on Iran's enrichment capability will not necessarily lead to greater transparency. Keeping thousands of centrifuges in place, many of them a flip of a switch away from becoming operational, would seriously complicate the IAEA's ability to monitor Iranian compliance. Separately, the Administration has relinquished its effort to shut off Iran's plutonium path to a bomb by converting its heavy water reactor at Arak to a light water reactor.

---

[9] For a typical example of Secretary Kerry's statements to this effect see his Interview with Rima Maktabi of al-Arabiya, January 23, 2014 at http://www.state.gov/secretary/remarks/2014/01/220559.htm, accessed January 24, 2015. As former Spanish President Jose Maria Aznar has noted, " Just about every Western leader is consistently on record regarding Iran's nuclear program, saying: 'No deal is better than a bad deal,'" *Wall Street Journal*, November 25, 2014.

The P5+1 also appears to have given up on full Iranian transparency on PMD as part and parcel of any final deal, even though as recently as September 2014 the IAEA said it "remains concerned about the possible existence in Iran of undisclosed nuclear related activities involving military related organizations, including activities related to the development of a nuclear payload for a missile."[10] Though Iran has provided information on certain aspects of the IAEA's inquiry, it still has not cooperated over its prior research on explosives for a nuclear warhead. Unless these issues are resolved to the IAEA's satisfaction beforehand, it will be hard to have any confidence that a final agreement will possess the kind of monitoring and verification mechanisms that would ensure Iran cannot develop a nuclear weapons capability. The consequences of U.S. acquiescence in a bad deal would reverberate, for the reasons outlined above, throughout the region and beyond in the rest of the world.

Reversing Course to an Acceptable Deal

It is difficult to envisage an acceptable agreement without a change in the trajectory of the negotiations, and with it a decisive change in Iran's calculus of its own best interests. Thus far the talks demonstrate Tehran's ability to exploit weakness in its opponents. That being said, the Iranian leadership also responds to pressure and the threat of force: it first agreed to suspend enrichment in 2003 out of fear that it was the next target of U.S. military action after the Taliban and Saddam Hussein, and it initially came back to the table in 2013 seeking to alleviate the pain of crippling sanctions.

---

[10] IAEA, "Implementation of the NPT Safeguards Agreement and relevant provisions of Security Council resolutions in the Islamic Republic of Iran," GOV/2014/43, September 5, 2014, p. 12.

Therefore, American policymakers must use all available instruments of coercive diplomacy to restore credibility to the oft-repeated statement that every option remains on the table to prevent a nuclear Iran. Success is possible only if Iran realizes it has the most to lose from the failure of diplomacy.

The United States retains a real ability to exert pressure through sanctions. Given the initial positive effects of sanctions relief for Iran under the interim deal, the Rouhani Administration is eager for a rapid and complete lifting of all remaining U.S. sanctions. Moreover, the current oil market balance is highly disadvantageous toward Iran. Not to put too fine a point on it, given the current price of oil the U.S. need not fear that absence of Iranian oil would roil the markets and set back the recovery of the global economy. For these reasons, the United States can credibly threaten more stringent measures against energy and other vital economic sectors if Iran continues its obstinacy.

Military options continue to be viable as well. The United States already has sufficient capability in-theater to carry out a military strike on Iran's nuclear-related facilities, but the deterrent credibility of that option also depends on the perceived U.S. willingness to execute it. American policymakers should clarify and strengthen their declaratory policy, including Congressional hearings on the feasibility of the U.S. military option and publicizing advanced U.S. military capabilities, such as the GBU-57 Massive Ordnance Penetrator (MOP) bunker buster designed specifically to reach targets like Iran's deeply-buried illegal nuclear facilities. Such activities will make it abundantly clear to Tehran that the United States can use military force as a last resort to prevent a nuclear Iran.

The United States should also boost the credibility of Israel's military option. Contrasted with the United States, which has the unquestioned capability but uncertain will to carry out such a strike, Israel's own capability may not match its determination to do so. Therefore, the United States could actively consider the value of generating additional leverage by transferring MOP bunker busters to Israel. Because Israel currently lacks aircraft to carry the MOP, the United States would need to consider transferring an appropriate delivery platform and additional tanking capability as well. Simply beginning a discussion of these options would bolster the U.S. position at the negotiating table by communicating our preparedness to consider other options if diplomacy continues to go nowhere.

Finally, the United States must be willing to compete with Iran, <u>rather than actively seeking its partnership.</u> On one level, this requires a change in tone. The Administration must emphasize its readiness to exert more pressure on Iran instead of exerting pressure on Congress with talking points that come "straight out of Tehran," according to a ranking member of the Senate.[11] On another level, the United States must respond more robustly to Tehran's ongoing efforts to shift the balance of power in the Middle East. Rather than asking its cooperation and blessing – especially in Iraq and Syria – the United States should undertake every possible effort to isolate Iran in its own backyard. By showing that the United States is willing to contest Iran's aspirations for hegemony it can magnify Iran's concerns about the costs of diplomacy's failure.[12]

---

[11] Cheryl K. Chumley, "Democrat Sen. Menendez: Obama's points on Iran come 'straight out of Tehran'," *Washington Times*, January 21, 2015.
[12] In this regard see Dennis Ross, Eric Edelman and Ray Takeyh, "Time to Take It to Iran," *Politico*, January 23, 2015

I thank the Chairman for scheduling this hearing and the members for their patience and consideration. Thank you.

Chairman ROYCE. Thank you, Ambassador. Mr. Hannah.

STATEMENT OF MR. JOHN HANNAH, SENIOR FELLOW, FOUNDATION FOR DEFENSE OF DEMOCRACIES

Mr. HANNAH. Thank you, Mr. Chairman. Mr. Chairman, Congressman Sherman, members of the committee, thank you for the opportunity to participate in this hearing. I have to confess to having deep concerns about the state of the negotiations with Iran. I worry that, starting with the Joint Plan of Action, the United States has already agreed to a series of concessions that will make the achievement of a good deal very difficult.

The decision 14 months ago to accede to Iran's core demand that it retain an ability to enrich uranium was indeed a fateful one. It reversed longstanding U.S. policy opposing any Iranian enrichment and contravened six hard-won U.N. Security Council resolutions. It represented a strategic concession by the United States on an issue of absolutely central importance to Iran. Whatever the merits of the Joint Plan of Action, and I agree with Congressman Sherman that it does have merits, the fact is that Iran was required to make no reciprocal concession of even remotely similar strategic value to the United States.

On the contrary, every commitment made by Iran under the JPOA has been strictly tactical in nature and easily reversible. The administration's concession on enrichment had the effect of transforming the fundamental objective of U.S. strategy toward Iran. It represented the abandonment of the goal of eliminating Iran's capability to produce nuclear weapons. Instead, the United States retreated to the much less ambitious goal of simply extending the time it would take Iran to break out to a nuclear bomb.

The concession on enrichment, unfortunately, set the template for what has been a troubling dynamic that has come to characterize the talks. On a number of key issues, virtually all the concessions have come from the P5+1. All the significant movement has been away from America's red lines and toward Iran's red lines. And in the process, in my view, the heart of America's longtime position with respect to Iran's nuclear program, that is, the dismantlement, destruction, and irreversible rollback of Iran's nuclear weapons-related infrastructure, has largely been gutted.

As problematic as this is, perhaps even more troubling is a second concession of enormous strategic consequence that the U.S. made to secure the JPOA. I am referring to the so-called sunset clause that put an expiration date on any comprehensive deal that might be reached. In short, whatever restrictions that a final deal imposes on Iran's nuclear program will themselves only be temporary.

After a period of years yet to be determined—the U.S. is hoping for 15—Iran will not only be free of all sanctions, it will be treated on a par with every other non-nuclear weapon state that is a member in good standing of the NPT. That means that Iran can be like The Netherlands, which spins hundreds of thousands of centrifuges to produce reactor fuel. It can be like Japan that maintains enough stockpiled plutonium for thousands of nuclear warheads. It can be like Brazil that plans to produce highly enriched uranium of up to 90 percent to power its nuclear submarines. All of that will be perfectly permissible—regardless of whether Iran in 15 years is led by the equivalent of Ahmadinejad 2.0; regardless of whether its highest political and military leaders continue to call for Israel's destruction; and regardless of whether Iran remains the world's leading sponsor of terrorism.

Some may hope that in those intervening 15 years Iran will be transformed into a normal, non-revolutionary power that is prepared to forego its war with the Great Satan and its ambitions to dominate the Middle East. Perhaps those hopes will be borne out. But who would be willing to bet U.S. national security on it? In my mind, that is an enormous risk to run.

I recognize, of course, that despite the very generous concessions that the P5+1 have put forward, Ayatollah Ali Khamenei's intransigence continues. We can speculate on why that is the case and what more might still be done to break the stalemate by convincing the Supreme Leader to make the concessions necessary for a deal, including the possibility of legislating prospective sanctions. But at the same time, I would simply urge that Congress devote at least as much energy to examining the substance of any deal that might emerge, with the aim of identifying those outstanding issues where Congress might still be able help to stiffen the administration's positions in ways that would mitigate the risks as much as possible.

Finding ways to increase pressure on Iran to make a deal is certainly a critical issue. But simply pressuring Iran for the purpose of accepting what could amount to a bad deal would be a pyrrhic victory, indeed. Thank you again for the opportunity to present my views and I look forward to your questions.

[The prepared statement of Mr. Hannah follows:]

Congressional Testimony

Iran Nuclear Negotiations After The Second Extension
Where Are They Going?

John Hannah
Senior Fellow
Foundation for Defense of Democracies

House Committee on Foreign Affairs

Washington, DC
January 27, 2015

FOUNDATION FOR
DEFENSE OF DEMOCRACIES   1726 M Street NW ● Suite 700 ● Washington, DC 20036

Mr. Chairman, Ranking Member Engel, Members of the Committee: Thank you for the opportunity to participate in this hearing.

I must confess to having deep concerns about the state of the negotiations with Iran.

I worry that, starting with the Joint Plan of Action (JPOA), the United States has already agreed to a series of concessions that will make the achievement of a good deal very difficult.

The decision 14 months ago to accede to Iran's core demand that it retain an ability to enrich uranium was indeed a fateful one.

It reversed longstanding U.S. policy opposing any Iranian enrichment and contravened six hard-won U.N. Security Council resolutions.

It represented a strategic concession by the United States on an issue of central importance to Iran.

Whatever the merits of the Joint Plan of Action, the fact is that Iran was required to make no reciprocal concession of even remotely similar strategic value to the United States.

On the contrary, every commitment made by Iran under the JPOA has been strictly tactical in nature and easily reversible.

The administration's concession on enrichment had the effect of transforming the fundamental objective of U.S. strategy toward Iran.

It represented the abandonment of the goal of eliminating Iran's capability to produce nuclear weapons.

Instead, the United States retreated to the much less ambitious goal of simply extending the time it would take Iran to break out to a nuclear bomb.

The concession on enrichment, unfortunately, set the template for a troubling dynamic that has come to characterize the talks.

On a number of key issues, virtually all the concessions have come from the P5+1.

All the significant movement has been away from America's red lines and towards Iran's red lines.

In the process, the heart of America's longtime position with respect to Iran's nuclear program -- that is, the dismantlement, destruction, and irreversible rollback of Iran's nuclear weapons-related infrastructure -- has largely been gutted.

As problematic as this is, perhaps even more troubling is a second concession of enormous strategic consequence that the U.S. made to secure the JPOA.

I'm referring to the so-called sunset clause that put an expiration date on any comprehensive deal that might be reached.

In short, whatever restrictions that a final deal imposes on Iran's nuclear program will themselves only be temporary.

After a period of years yet to be determined -- the U.S. is hoping for 15 -- Iran will not only be free of all sanctions, it will be treated on a par with every other non-nuclear weapon state that is a member in good standing of the NPT (Nuclear Non-Proliferation Treaty).

That means that Iran can be like Holland, which spins hundreds of thousands of centrifuges to produce reactor fuel.

It can be like Japan that maintains enough stockpiled plutonium for thousands of nuclear warheads.

It can be like Brazil that plans to produce highly enriched uranium of up to 90 percent to power its nuclear submarines.

All of that will be perfectly permissible -- regardless of whether Iran in 15 years is led by the equivalent of Ahmadinejad 2.0; regardless of whether its highest political and military leaders continue to call for Israel's destruction; and regardless of whether Iran remains the world's leading state sponsor of terrorism.

Some may hope that in those intervening 15 years Iran will be transformed into a normal, non-revolutionary power that is prepared to forego its war with the Great Satan and its ambitions to dominate the Middle East.

Perhaps those hopes will be borne out. But who would be willing to bet U.S. national security on it? That's an enormous risk to run.

I recognize, of course, that despite the very generous concessions the P5+1 have put forward, Ayatollah Ali Khamenei's intransigence continues.

We can speculate on why that's the case and what more might still be done to break the stalemate by convincing the Supreme Leader to make the concessions necessary for a deal -- including the possibility of legislating prospective sanctions.

But at the same time I would simply urge that Congress devote at least as much energy to examining the substance of any deal that might emerge, with the aim of identifying those outstanding issues where Congress might still help to stiffen the administration's position in ways that would mitigate the risks as much as possible.

Finding ways to increase pressure on Iran to make a deal is certainly critical. But simply pressuring Iran for the purpose of accepting what could amount to a bad deal would be a pyrrhic victory, indeed.

Thank you again for this opportunity to present my views. I look forward to your questions.

STATEMENT OF MR. RAY TAKEYH, SENIOR FELLOW FOR MIDDLE EASTERN STUDIES, COUNCIL ON FOREIGN RELATIONS

Mr. TAKEYH. Thank you, members of the committee, for inviting me to come back once more. I would echo actually what Chairman Royce suggested, namely that the nuclear negotiations between Iran and the P5+1 are today stalemated after a decade of patient diplomacy. I think the prospect of securing a final deal is becoming increasingly remote. The wheels of diplomacy will grind on. There have been two extensions already granted. But it is time to acknowledge that the policy of engagement as pursued over the past decade was predicated on a series of assumptions that have proven logical in concept, but flawed in practice.

As we reassess our next move, it will be wise to reconsider the judgments that underwrite our approach to an adversary that has, at the very least, proven rather elusive.

I would say successive administrations have relied solely on financial stress to temper Iran's ambitions, nuclear and otherwise. At the core, this policy argues for steady economic pressure to change the calculus of the Islamic Republic, eventually leading it to concede the most disturbing aspects of its nuclear program. This was American pragmatism at its most obvious, as economics is thought to transcend ideology and history in conditioning national priorities. To be sure, the policy has not been without its successes, as it solidified a sanctions regime that compelled Iran to change its negotiating style. Still, what was missed was that the Islamic Republic is a revolutionary state that rarely makes judicious economic decisions. In fact, the notion of integration into the global economy is frightening to the regime's highly ideological rulers, who require an external nemesis to justify their hegemony power.

Among other assumptions that I think we have misdiagnosed is the changes in Iran's political landscape since 2009. The fraudulent 2009 Presidential election, in my view, was not a passing event, but a watershed moment. Watershed moment means after which things are very different than anything that went before. Iran today is a government very similar to other Middle Eastern dictatorships. The forces of reform have been purged from body politic, leaving behind like-minded actors.

While many in the West continue to see Iran as a country of quarreling factions and competing personalities, the Iranians themselves talk of the system. This is not to suggest that there are no disagreements among key actors, but the system has forged the rough consensus on issues such as repressing dissent at home, pursuing an aggressive policy abroad, and even sustaining the essential trajectory of the nuclear program. The U.S. misdiagnosis was most glaring, in my view, when Hassan Rouhani assumed the presidency in 2013. Rouhani's election was considered a rebuke to Supreme Leader Ali Khamenei and his ideological presumptions, and many in Washington convinced themselves that by investing in Rouhani they could usher in an age of moderation in Iran. Suddenly, an empowered Rouhani would make important concessions on the nuclear issue and even collaborate with the United States to steady an unhinged region. Again, missing from all this is how the system had come together in the aftermath of 2009, to destroy the democratic left. We have sought to manipulate Iran's factions at the precise time when factionalism is no longer the defining aspect of Iranian politics.

Yet another American misapprehension was refusing to listen to what the Iranians were actually saying. The United States has offered Iran a number of concessions such as the recognition of its enrichment and practice. It was hoped that those concessions would cause Iran to settle for a modest program. Thus symbolic offerings from the West would diminish Iran's expansive nuclear appetite. In this case, we refused to listen to what Iranians were saying, namely that they want an industrial-size nuclear program in public and private. Thus far, we have made concessions in that particular sense.

Iran will not easily be deterred from its approach. A strategy of coercion must move beyond imposing financial penalties as Chairman Royce suggested. Iran must feel pressure on many fronts. The Obama administration, in my view, would be wise to mend fences at home and rehabilitate our better alliances in the Middle East. It is important for Iran to see no division in its efforts to exploit the differences between the White House and the Congress. The President would be wise to consult with Congress on various legislation moving forward. Both parties have equities that need to be taken into consideration. I think they can be in a genuine conversation between the Executive and Legislative Branches.

Finally, let me say, there is nothing magical about the July deadline. If there is an agreement by July, Iran will be left with a substantial nuclear infrastructure that is destined to grow over time. If there is no agreement in July, Iran will be left with a substantial nuclear infrastructure that is destined to grow over time, perhaps at an unsteady pace. Therefore, we need to develop a long-term strategy for developing how to maintain, contain, regulate Iran with nuclear material that is substantial and growing. And that is a long-term challenge that I think the Executive Branch and Congress can come together and actually craft. Thank you.

[The prepared statement of Mr. Takeyh follows:]

COUNCIL on
FOREIGN
RELATIONS

1777 F Street, NW, Washington, DC 20006
tel 202.509.8400 fax 202.509.8490 www.cfr.org

Iran Nuclear Negotiations After the Second Extension: Where Are They Going?

Prepared Statement by

Ray Takeyh
Senior Fellow for Middle East Studies, Council on Foreign Relations

Before the
Committee of Foreign Affairs
United States House of Representatives

The nuclear negotiations between the United States and Iran are stalemated. After a decade of patient talks, the prospect of the United States and other powers securing a final agreement are not good. The wheels of diplomacy will grind on and two extensions of the talks have already been granted. But it is time to acknowledge that the policy of engagement was predicated on a serious of assumptions that, although logical, have proven largely incorrect. As we assess our next move, it would be wise to reconsider the judgments that have underwritten our approach to one of our most elusive adversaries.

Successive administrations have relied solely on financial stress to temper Iran's nuclear ambitions. At core, this policy has argued that steady economic pressure would change the calculus of the Islamic Republic, eventually leading it to concede the most disturbing aspects of its nuclear program. This was American pragmatism at its most obvious, as economics is thought to transcend ideology and history in conditioning national priorities. To be sure, the policy has not been without its successes, as it solidified a sanctions regime that compelled Iran to change its negotiating style. Still, what was missed was that the Islamic Republic is a revolutionary state that rarely makes judicious economic decisions. In fact, the notion of integration into the global economy is frightening to Iran's highly ideological rulers, who require an external enemy to justify their absolutist rule.

Washington's diplomatic strategies seemed to be equally uninformed by the changing dynamics of Iranian politics. The fraudulent 2009 presidential election was a watershed even in Iran's history, as it transformed the Islamic Republic from a government of factions into just another Middle Eastern dictatorship. The forces of reform were purged from the body politic, leaving behind any like-minded mullahs. While many in the West see Iran as a country of quarrelling factions and competing personalities, the Iranians themselves talk of nezam—the system. This is not to suggest that there are no disagreements among key actors, but the system has forged a rough consensus on issues such as repressing dissent and preserving the essential trajectory of the nuclear program.

The U.S. misdiagnosis of Iran was at its most glaring when Hassan Rouhani assumed the presidency in 2013. Rouhani's election was considered a rebuke to Supreme Leader Ali Khamenei and his ideological presumptions, and many in Washington convinced themselves that by investing in Rouhani they could usher in an age of moderation in Iran. Suddenly, an empowered Rouhani would make important concessions on the nuclear issue and even collaborate with the United States to steady an unhinged region. Missing from all this was how the system had come together in 2009, consolidated its power and destroyed the democratic left. The Obama administration sought to manipulate Iran's factions at the precise moment when factionalism was no longer the defining aspect of Iranian politics.

Yet another American misapprehension was refusing to listen to what the Iranians were actually saying. The United States perceived that by offering Iran concessions such as the recognition of its right to enrich, Tehran would settle for a modest program. Thus symbolic offerings from the West would diminish Iran's expansive nuclear appetite. In this sense, we seemed to have willfully ignored the persistent Iranian claim that they required an industrial-size nuclear program and in quick order. Today, we find ourselves in a difficult situation of having conceded on important issues—such as the right to enrich—without comparable Iranian compromises.

Although there is little evidence that the Western powers are contemplating alternative strategies, important actors in Iran are beginning to consider life after diplomatic failure. During the past few years, Khamenei has been pressing his concept of resistance economy whereby Iran would shed its need for foreign contracts and commerce. "Instead of reliance on oil revenues, Iran should be managed through reliance on its internal forces and the resources on the ground," insisted Khamenei. In the impractical universe of conservatives, Iran can meet the basic needs of its people by developing local industries. Iran's reactionaries seem to prefer national poverty to nuclear disarmament.

The notions of self-sufficiency and self-reliance have long been hallmarks of conservative thinking in Iran. Since the 1980s, the central tenant of the hardliners foreign policy perspective has been that Iran's revolution is a remarkable historical achievement that the United States cannot accept or accommodate. Western powers will always conspire against an Islamic state that they cannot control, this thinking goes, and the only way Iran can secure its independence and achieve its national objectives is to lessen its reliance on its principal export commodity. Hardliners believe that isolation from the international community can best preserve Iran's ideological identity. This siege mentality drives Iran's quest for nuclear arms and their deterrent power.

Although many are concerned about the longevity of the negotiations should the Congress enact various legislations, it is important to stress that the Islamic Republic is deeply invested in the negotiating process for its own reasons. While the United States sees nuclear diplomacy as advancing the cause of détente and arms control, Iran sees it as yet another shield to hide its ominous policies.

Since the exposure of its illicit nuclear program in 2002, Iran's main intention has been to legitimize its expanding nuclear infrastructure. The record shows that Iran's diplomats have gone far in achieving that objective. Although numerous United Nations Security Council resolutions have enjoined Iran to suspend all of its nuclear activities, there is little interest by the great powers in enforcing the injunctions they crafted in the first place. Last year's interim accord—the Joint Plan of Action—not only acknowledged Iran's right to enrich uranium at home but also stipulated that, after a period of time, enrichment capacity could be industrialized. These are impressive accomplishments for a state that not only defies the U.N. Security Council but also thwarts the International Atomic Energy Agency's attempt to gain access to its scientists and sites. So long as Iran stays at the table it can count on further Western indulgences.

Iran has also gained much in non-nuclear sectors from its continued participation in the talks. Its dismal human rights record and harsh repression of its citizens are rarely mentioned by the

Western chancelleries. A standard practice of America's Cold War summitry was to press the cause of dissidents in encounters with Soviet representatives. Given fears that Iran's hyper-sensitive mullahs would abjure nuclear compromises should their domestic abuses be highlighted, Western diplomats have been largely silent about Iran's domestic shortcomings. The nuclear talks and the prospects of an accord conveniently shield the Iranian supreme leader, Ayatollah Ali Khamenei, and his penal colony from censure and criticism.

In the region, Iran's aggressive policies remain largely unaddressed given its participation in the nuclear talks. Through its proxies and aid Iran is propping up the Bashar Assad government in Syria and enabling its war against its citizens. Iran is the most consequential external actor in Iraq and has been instrumental in pressing its Shia allies to reject substantial inclusion of Sunni Muslims in Iraq's government. The ominous shadow of Iran hangs over the disorder sweeping Yemen, as the Islamic Republic has long been the benefactor of those who have successfully battled the central government. And Iran's lethal Hezbollah protégé is now operating ominously close to Israeli boundaries.

All the curiosity of America's policy were on display in a letter reportedly sent by President Obama to Khamenei offering to work with Iran in disarming the militant group, the Islamic State. Such correspondence misses the point that Iran has already rejected collaboration with the United States on regional affairs and that its leaders have claimed that America created Islamic State as a means of justifying its return to Iraq.

Iran will not easily alter its approach and our strategy of coercion must move beyond imposing financial penalties. Iran must fact pressure across many fronts, and the Obama administration should focus on mending fences at home while rehabilitating our battered alliances in the Middle East. It is important for Tehran to see that there are no divisions for it to exploit between the White House and Congress. The president would be wise to consult with Congress on various legislations making their way through the hill. Both parties have concerns that can best be addressed through a process of genuine dialogue between the two branches of government. The White House should appreciate that any agreement that does not have the support the Congress is unlikely to survive the Obama presidency.

A new strategy of pressure should also focus on isolating Iran in its neighborhood and undermining its clients. This will necessitate U.S. involvement in the region's many crises. For both humanitarian and strategic reasons, the United States must be invested in the outcome of the

Syrian civil war and change the balance of power in that hapless country. Similarly, the Iraqi government must be pressured into limiting Iran's influence. It is unlikely that Baghdad will move in that direction as long as our campaign against the Islamic State remains hesitant and we hint at possible collaboration with Iran there. The core of the U.S. alliance system in the Middle East remains our close partnership with Israel. The value of U.S. deterrence is not enhanced by perceptions of discord in that essential relationship.

The purpose of this new, robust and coercive strategy is to signal our readiness to compete, to show that we don't need a deal more than Iran does and to raise the price to Tehran of its objectionable policies. It is time to press the Iranians to make the tough choices that they have been unwilling to make.

The United States and Iran are destined to remain adversaries. Beyond the nuclear issue, the Islamic Republic continues to rely on terrorism as an essential instrument of its foreign policy. From the Levant to the Persian Gulf, Iran, Iran and its proxies are busy undermining our allies and promoting their agents. Irrespective of the ebbs and flows of nuclear diplomacy, we should continue to focus our efforts on ways of limiting Iran's aggressive policies in the Middle East.

Chairman ROYCE. Thank you, Doctor. Mr. Einhorn?

STATEMENT OF THE HONORABLE ROBERT EINHORN, SENIOR FELLOW, FOREIGN POLICY PROGRAM, THE BROOKINGS INSTITUTION

Mr. EINHORN. Chairman Royce, Congressman Sherman, other distinguished members of the committee, I want to thank you for this opportunity to testify on the Iran nuclear issue.

The Obama administration is seeking an agreement that would lengthen to at least 1 year the time it would take Iran to produce enough nuclear material for a single nuclear weapon. It is also seeking rigorous monitoring measures that would enable the IAEA to detect at the earliest possible time any Iranian attempt to break out of an agreement at either declared or covert locations. The goal is to make Iran's potential path to nuclear weapons lengthy and readily detectable so that the United States and others would have plenty of time to intervene decisively in order to stop them, using economic or military means.

Negotiations between Iran and the P5+1 countries have made significant progress over the last year. But Iran has showed little flexibility on some central issues, including enrichment capacity and the duration of any comprehensive agreement. So it is understandable that many Members of Congress support new sanctions to pressure the Iranians to accept the compromises needed to make a deal possible.

I agree that economic pressure brought the Iranians to the negotiating table and continued strong pressure will be essential to get them to accept an agreement that meets U.S. requirements. But enacting new sanctions legislation at this time, even if sanctions would not be imposed until a later date, could have the unintended effect of hardening Iran's negotiating position and weakening international sanctions.

Iranians are sharply divided on the nuclear issue. Opponents of a deal would seize on any new U.S. sanctions legislation to claim that the United States has no intention of ultimately removing sanctions. They would argue internally that an agreement would therefore be pointless and they would oppose Iranian flexibility in the negotiations. So even if the Iranians don't walk out of the talks as they have threatened to do, new sanctions legislation could reinforce Iranian rigidity and increase the likelihood that negotiations will fail.

New sanctions legislation could also undermine the unity of the International Sanctions Coalition. So far that coalition has stayed together because Iran has been seen as the main impediment to the negotiations. Key countries would regard new sanctions as premature and unnecessarily provocative. The blame for any impasse or breakdown could shift to us and support for tough sanctions could begin to unravel. Not only is the new legislation potentially counterproductive in terms of Iran's negotiating posture and the unity of international sanctions efforts, it is unnecessary.

Iran continues to feel immense economic pressure from existing sanctions which remain intact under the Joint Plan of Action and the steep drop in the price of oil serves as an additional sanction, depriving Iran's economy of another $11 billion over the next 6 months. Under the interim deal, Iran each month receives $700 million of its own oil revenues that have been held in restricted overseas accounts. Compare that to the $40 billion in oil revenues that Iran lost in 2014 because of the sanctions.

So if new sanctions legislation is neither necessary, nor likely to have its intended effect, how can we get the Iranians to accept a nuclear deal that meets our requirements? First, we should be patient. Our negotiators should continue to work toward concluding a deal along the lines we have already proposed by the June deadline. But they need not be in a rush. If Iran remains reluctant to compromise, the U.S. and the P5+1 partners can afford to wait. Some have argued that the interim deal is advantageous to Iran, that the Iranians are stringing us along, using the interim deal to play for time. I find this argument hard to understand. Under the JPOA, Iran's nuclear program is frozen in most meaningful respects. And Iran's economy continues to suffer under punishing sanctions, amplified now by the drop in the price of oil.

It is Iran, not the United States, that is the clear loser the longer the JPOA remains in effect. No one wants to prolong the negotiations indefinitely, but if a sound agreement cannot be reached by the end of June, the option of another extension should not be ruled out.

Second, the administration should do whatever it can to maintain and enhance the effectiveness of existing sanctions. The Treasury Department should continue its aggressive efforts to remind governments and companies around the world that sanctions remain in place and that Iran is not open for business.

Third, even while negotiations are underway, the administration should work with the Congress and its foreign partners on a Plan B, a plan for the eventuality that no agreement will be reached. The Legislative and Executive Branches should begin now to jointly develop sanctions legislation that would be ready to be voted and immediately implemented in the event that the talks end without agreement. The administration should also begin now to consult key foreign partners on the ratcheting up of sanctions as well as on the strengthening of cooperative defense plans that may be warranted in the event of a breakdown of negotiations.

Of course, it is impossible to know whether Iran will eventually come around to the realization that without a nuclear deal its economy will continue to suffer and its international isolation will persist. President Obama puts the odds at less than 50–50. If we cannot achieve an agreement that meets our requirements, then we will have little choice but to turn from diplomacy to other means of preventing Iran from acquiring nuclear weapons. And if diplomacy fails, it is critical that we have the strong international support necessary for whatever course we decide to take. We should therefore avoid actions at the present time that would widely be seen as undermining prospects for an agreement. Thank you, Mr. Chairman.

[The prepared statement of Mr. Einhorn follows:]

HOUSE COMMITTEE ON FOREIGN AFFAIRS

"Iran Nuclear Negotiations After the Second Extension:
Where Are They Going?"
January 27, 2015

Written Statement by Robert J. Einhorn
The Brookings Institution

Chairman Royce, Ranking Member Engel, and other Members of the Committee, thank you for giving me the opportunity to share my thoughts on the Iran nuclear issue.

With the Iran nuclear negotiations now well into their second extension period, no one can confidently predict that a comprehensive agreement will eventually be reached. President Obama speaks of less than a 50 percent chance of success. While some significant progress has been achieved over the last year, wide gaps remain on some central issues.

Requirements of a sound comprehensive agreement

To meet its goal of preventing Iran from acquiring a nuclear weapon, the Obama Administration is seeking an agreement that would lengthen to at least one year the time it would take Iran to produce enough nuclear material for a single nuclear weapon, should it decide to leave or violate the agreement. A one-year "breakout" time would require Iran to reduce substantially its current operational centrifuge enrichment capability as well as to cap the amount of low-enriched uranium stocks on its territory at a low level. To block the plutonium path to a bomb, Iran would have to re-design its Arak reactor to lower its production of plutonium to such a small amount that breakout would be infeasible.

To deter and detect violations at both declared and covert locations, the deal would have to provide for rigorous monitoring measures that go well beyond the IAEA's Additional Protocol, and it would require Iran to resolve concerns about its past activities that the IAEA suspects were related to nuclear weapons development. And to build confidence that Iran's nuclear program is peaceful, the agreement would need to have a duration of about 15 years.

A key Iranian goal is the early removal of U.N., U.S., and European Union sanctions. To meet U.S. requirements, the suspension and eventual lifting of sanctions would have to be timed to coincide with Iran's performance in implementing agreed constraints on its nuclear program as well as with the IAEA's conclusions regarding Iran's compliance with its obligations.

Some observers, in the U.S. and abroad, have called for an agreement obliging Iran to abandon key elements of its nuclear program – for example, an agreement banning enrichment altogether and requiring the dismantlement of enrichment facilities and the Arak reactor. Such an agreement would be ideal. But no one who closely follows Iran and its domestic politics believes that it is achievable, whatever pressures we are able to bring to bear. Iranian leaders have successfully convinced their public that an enrichment capability is an inalienable right, an essential component of a respectable civil nuclear program, and a source of national pride – and that giving it up in the face of Western pressure would be a national humiliation. No one across the Iranian political spectrum, even those who strongly want a deal, would be prepared to accept an outcome banning enrichment and dismantling nuclear facilities.

But we don't need such an ideal but unattainable agreement to protect our national security and that of our partners in the Middle East. An agreement along the lines that the United States and its P5+1 partners are seeking – one that would allow a strictly limited and heavily monitored enrichment program – could also prevent Iran from acquiring nuclear weapons. It could do so by making it clear to future Iranian leaders that the time it would take them to build a nuclear weapon is long, that efforts to break out at declared or covert locations would be detected at an early date, and that the United States and others in the international community would have plenty of time to intervene decisively to stop them, through diplomatic or economic pressures or the use of military force.

Alternatives to a negotiated deal

In evaluating any deal that may emerge from negotiations, it is import to compare it not with the best deal we can possibly imagine but with the realistic alternatives to a negotiated solution. One alternative is to try to continue ratcheting up economic pressures until Iran accedes to our demands. But it is unclear the extent to which we could command the necessary international support for dramatically strengthened sanctions, and it is unclear whether even such strengthened sanctions could compel Iran's acceptance of our demands.

Another alternative is military force. Military force could set back Iran's nuclear program. But such a setback would probably only be temporary, and the use of force could trigger an Iranian decision to go for nuclear weapons as soon as possible, a decision that we believe has so far been deferred. Moreover, with IAEA inspectors evicted, we would lose our best window into Iran's program and, at least as important, we would lose the international support we would need to keep pressure on Iran in the post-attack environment.

The United States may eventually decide that the deal Iran is willing to accept does not meet essential U.S. requirements. In that case, the Administration will have little choice but to pursue these non-diplomatic alternatives. But in evaluating whether an attainable deal is good enough, it is essential to have a clear-eyed view of the alternatives to a negotiated solution.

Iran's reluctance to compromise

If Iran is truly interested in pursuing a civil nuclear energy program, the deal the P5+1 countries are offering should be acceptable. The limited enrichment program that would be permitted would enable Iran to provide fuel for one or two research reactors; it could continue importing fuel from Russia for the Bushehr power reactor or any additional power reactors it buys from Russia; and in the long term, once the agreement has expired, it would have the freedom to increase its enrichment capacity to promote its ambitious future nuclear energy goals. And critical to the Iranian economy, sanctions would be suspended at an early date as Iran meets implementation milestones and eventually would be lifted, with Congressional approval, as the IAEA concludes that Iran's program is peaceful.

But so far, Iran has not been willing to accept such an approach. It has resisted all but a very modest reduction in its current centrifuge enrichment capacity, and it favors a relatively short-duration agreement that would allow it to ramp up its enrichment program to industrial scale (more than ten times its current operational capacity) at an early date. It has also been reluctant to permit inspector access to military installations or to accept monitoring measures beyond the Additional Protocol.

Although Iran has been prepared to compromise on some important issues – including to reduce the plutonium production capacity of the Arak reactor, re-purpose the Fordow enrichment facility, and ship most of its low-enriched uranium stocks to Russia – its rigidity on central issues such as enrichment capacity and duration made it impossible to come to agreement before the deadline of the last extension period on November 24th.

We can only speculate why Iran has not been prepared to compromise on these central issues. In the run-up to the November deadline, Iran may have seen itself in a strong position and felt that it only needed to wait until the United States and its partners accepted a deal largely on its terms. It may have calculated that the U.S. would make concessions on the nuclear issue to gain Iran's cooperation in defeating the Islamic State and in addressing other regional issues. It may have figured that President Obama was anxious to conclude a deal before the Republicans took over the Senate. By the end of the November negotiating round, when U.S. negotiators stood their ground, the Iranians presumably learned that such calculations were wrong.

A more fundamental explanation is that deep internal divisions within Iran – not just on the contents of an agreement but on the very idea of an agreement – have prevented the adoption of a pragmatic Iranian negotiating posture. Some in Iran support an agreement and believe it is needed to alleviate Iran's economic plight. Some others claim Iran can manage economically without an agreement and are only willing to support a deal largely on Iran's terms. Still others oppose any deal, believing it would threaten Iran's revolutionary ideals and, for some individuals and entities, could prevent them from exploiting the sanctions for their own economic benefit.

President Rouhani has spoken out publicly in support of a nuclear agreement, arguing that the lifting of sanctions and ending of Iran's economic isolation are essential if its economy is to recover. But the ultimate decision-maker will be Supreme Leader Khamenei, and he seems deeply skeptical of the value of an agreement. He frequently states that the West cannot be trusted to remove sanctions, and he therefore favors an "economy of resistance," which he claims would rely on Iran's domestic resources and enable Iran to manage economically without an agreement or the lifting of sanctions.

Of course, a further explanation for Iran's reluctance to scale back its existing program and its insistence on being able to expand its program rapidly at an early date may be its desire to preserve a nuclear weapons option. The U.S. Intelligence Community continues to believe that a decision on whether to pursue nuclear weapons has not yet been taken, but it judges that Iran wants to keep its options open for the future. Iranian advocates of nuclear weapons may believe that an agreement that ensures a rapid breakout time, avoids intrusive monitoring, and has a short duration would keep that option more alive than one that substantially lengthens breakout time, provides for rigorous monitoring, and has a long duration – an outcome they may regard as effectively burning their bridges to acquiring nuclear weapons.

But whatever the explanation or combination of explanations, Iran will have to adopt a more realistic and pragmatic approach to the negotiations if agreement on the major elements of a deal is to be reached by March and a final deal is to be concluded by the end of June.

Interim deal favors the United States and its partners

The stepped-up pace of negotiations since the most recent extension was agreed in November – with several meetings between Secretary Kerry and Foreign Minister Zarif – suggests that all parties are genuinely interested in reaching a comprehensive deal by June at the latest. But while no party would like to see the Joint Plan of Action (JPOA) extended indefinitely or become permanent, the current interim arrangements appear much more favorable to the United States and its P5+1 partners than to Iran.

When the JPOA was concluded in November 2013, a number of observers, especially Israel, condemned the deal on the grounds that Iran would not abide by the constraints on its nuclear program and the JPOA's modest sanctions relief measures would lead to the unraveling of the sanctions regime. These predictions never materialized. The IAEA has repeatedly reported that Iran has complied with its JPOA commitments, and the most consequential sanctions, including on banking and oil, have remained intact.

Still, critics of the JPOA and of the negotiations continue to argue that the interim deal is in Iran's interest, claiming that Iran is "playing for time" and "stringing us along." In their view, the JPOA has not really halted Iran's nuclear program and has allowed Tehran to strengthen its economy. But this assessment is deeply flawed.

The JPOA has stopped forward movement in Iran's nuclear program in most critical respects. Iran is no longer producing 20 percent enriched uranium and has eliminated all 20 percent uranium hexafluoride by diluting it or converting it to oxide or fuel rods. Its stock of enriched uranium hexafluoride below 5 percent is capped at the November 2013 level. It has not installed or operated any additional centrifuges, and has not produced more centrifuges except to replace broken ones. Its centrifuge research and development program is strictly limited to prevent advancement to the next level of performance for each model. Meaningful progress toward operation of the Arak reactor has been blocked by banning the production or testing of fuel and the installation of additional reactor components.

Critics claim there are areas in which Iran's program can advance despite the JPOA. They point out, for example, that enriched uranium below 5 percent that is turned into oxide can be turned back into gas in violation of the agreement in a few weeks. They note that, even though the JPOA prevents certain advanced centrifuges from being installed or tested realistically with gas, it doesn't ban more preliminary R&D work (i.e., mechanical testing) without gas. And they say the JPOA doesn't prevent Iran from illicitly procuring equipment for the Arak reactor or from proceeding with some site construction work that does not involve the installation of key components.

It is true that there are some activities that Iran has continued under the JPOA. But these activities are relatively minor. In most consequential respects, Iran's program has been frozen. Iran has not been able to take meaningful steps toward shortening its breakout capability. Indeed, because of the JPOA, particularly the neutralization of the 20 percent stockpile, Iran's breakout time has increased. In the absence of the JPOA, the expansion of the program would have reduced the breakout time to a matter of a few weeks.

Moreover, because the JPOA calls for more frequent IAEA inspections of enrichment plants and gives the IAEA access to centrifuge production facilities, uranium mines and mills, and other key locations, the interim arrangements provide the international community a much better window into Iranian nuclear activities than we would otherwise have.

The argument that the JPOA has led to an erosion of sanctions and reduced economic pressures against Iran is sharply contradicted by the facts. Although companies around the world have held discussions with Iran in the hope of entering or re-entering the Iranian market, they are taking a very cautious approach, waiting for a nuclear deal to be concluded and sanctions to be removed before taking the risk of signing new contracts. With all consequential sanctions intact, Iran is still not a place where reputable banks and companies want to do business.

Under JPOA's sanctions relief measures, Iran has received $700 million per month of its own oil revenues that had been frozen in overseas restricted accounts. But these repatriated funds are a small fraction of the losses Iran continues to suffer from the sanctions. The Treasury Department estimates that in 2014, oil sanctions alone deprived Iran of about $40 billion in oil revenues, and that over the next six months it will lose another $15 billion. The recent sharp decline in oil prices is the equivalent of a major new sanction on Iran. Treasury Undersecretary David Cohen recently testified that, in the course of the current extension period, the drop in oil price will mean an additional loss of $11 billion.

While President Rouhani's economic team has adopted more effective policies than those of his predecessor, the Iranian economy as a whole remains in very bad shape. After a few years of a contracting GDP, Iran's per capita GDP is at least $1200 lower today than the $7000 per capita figure in 2012. The Iranian currency, the rial, has declined by about 56 percent since January 2012 and by about 16 percent since the JPOA was signed in November 2013. Inflation has come down somewhat since Rouhani took office, but remains high at 17 percent.

So it is hard to understand why the Iranians would have any incentive to play for time or string us along by prolonging the negotiations. They are the ones whose nuclear program has been frozen. They are the ones whose economy continues to suffer under punishing sanctions and now the steep drop in oil prices. No one wants to prolong the negotiations and the interim arrangements indefinitely. But there should be little doubt that it is Iran, not the United States or its partners, that is the clear loser the longer the JPOA remains in effect.

The likely effects of new sanctions legislation

Many in Congress believe that current economic pressures against Iran are not enough and that, in order to compel Tehran to adopt a more forthcoming position in the negotiations, it is necessary to legislate additional sanctions. One widely supported approach is to adopt tough new sanctions that would be imposed only if there is no agreement at the end of the current extension period or if Iran violates the interim agreement.

Proponents of new sanctions legislation are right that economic pressure brought Iran to the negotiating table and that continuing pressure will be essential to get Tehran to accept reasonable compromises. But enacting new sanctions legislation at this time – even sanctions that would not be imposed until a future date – would likely have the opposite effect than what the proponents intend. It could weaken the overall sanctions regime and produce not a softening but a hardening of the Iranian negotiating position.

Iranian officials have stated that new sanctions would mean a halt to the current negotiating process. It is hard to know whether Iran would actually follow through with that threat. It might decide to leave the talks or it might decide to continue them, perhaps after the Majlis had adopted its own tit-for-tat legislation requiring a resumption or expansion of currently-frozen nuclear activity if no agreement is reached by June.

But just as troublesome as the risk of an Iranian walkout is the impact new U.S. sanctions legislation would have on the internal debate in Tehran and on prospects for positive changes in Iran's negotiating position. Opponents of a deal would seize on the new legislation to argue that the United States is violating the spirit of the JPOA, that the U.S. has no intention of ultimately removing the sanctions, and that the U.S. Administration cannot be counted on to deliver its end of any agreement eventually reached. The critics – whose strong influence has so far impeded the adoption of a pragmatic Iranian negotiating position – would be further strengthened. Playing on Iranian hyper-sensitivity to giving in to foreign pressures, they would demand that U.S. pressure tactics not be rewarded by making concessions in the talks. Thus, instead of compelling Iran to be more flexible, new U.S. legislation could produce greater defiance, further entrench rigid Iranian negotiating positions, and increase support for the Supreme Leader's pipedream of an "economy of resistance" that could manage effectively without a nuclear deal. So even if a new sanctions law did not precipitate an abrupt termination of the talks, it could increase the likelihood that the negotiations will ultimately fail.

Not only would a new sanction law be counterproductive in terms of its goal of altering Iran's negotiating position; it could also have a very negative impact on the unity of the international sanctions coalition. Until now, that coalition has stayed together and continued to implement strong sanctions because it saw the Iranians as the main impediment to a deal. Key countries would regard new legislation as unnecessarily provocative and as putting at risk prospects for a successful negotiated solution. The blame for any impasse or breakdown could shift from Iran to the United States – a shift that Iran's active public diplomacy machine would be eager to encourage. More and more countries could be expected to relax their implementation of sanctions, and the overall sanctions regime could begin to unravel.

Moreover, the extent to which new sanctions legislation would actually result in stronger economic pressure is unclear. In recent years, the United States has been very successful in persuading foreign governments and companies to go along with U.S. sanctions, sometimes at considerable economic sacrifice to themselves. In particular, key countries like China, India, Japan, and South Korea were willing to cut way back on their purchases of Iranian crude oil, reducing their imports by as much as 50 percent or even more. But some of these countries have been warning the United States that they will resist cutting back further. Especially if new U.S. legislation is seen as having a disruptive effect on the talks, new sanctions requiring Iran's crude oil customers to reduce by at least an additional 30 percent or even to end all purchases could well fall on deaf ears. Instead of putting more pressure on Iran, we could find ourselves in high-profile disputes with key partner countries, threatening them with sanctions for violating our law.

If Iran remains unwilling to make the compromises needed to conclude an agreement and if negotiations break down as a result, it will be essential to ratchet up sanctions to a significantly higher level. But our ability to do that would be seriously impaired if we had fractured the international sanctions coalition by prematurely enacting new sanctions legislation.

So adopting a new sanctions law at the present time is very risky. But it is also unnecessary. With existing sanctions still in place – and their devastating effects further amplified by the drop in oil prices – Iran remains under intense economic pressure. As time passes, it will become harder and harder for Iranian opponents of a nuclear deal to make the case that Iran's economy can recover, or even muddle through, without an agreement.

If Tehran nonetheless remains unwilling or unable to make the compromises necessary to reach a deal and the talks break down, then the Congress, with the support of the Administration, can move very quickly to adopt and begin implementing new sanctions. The Iranians fully expect that this will happen. There is no need to legislate those sanctions in advance in order to ensure their credibility.

The current situation is frustrating. The United States has put forward reasonable proposals, but the Iranians are not showing sufficient flexibility – and the talks drag on. Because sanctions helped bring Iran to the negotiating table and induced them to begin negotiating seriously, it is understandable to assume that still more sanctions will produce the desired result. But given the dynamics of Iranian domestic politics, adopting new sanctions legislation now would probably only harden the Iranian negotiating position. And if legislative action is perceived internationally as undermining the talks, it could end up eroding the sanctions regime that the legislation was designed to strengthen.

What should be done?

Under these circumstances, how should the United States proceed? First, we should be patient. Our negotiators should continue to explore creative ways of persuading Iran to accept a deal that meets our essential requirements, and they should continue to seek an early conclusion, if possible, well before the late June deadline. But they need not be in a rush. If Iran remains reluctant to compromise, the United States and its P5+1 partners can afford to wait. After all, the current interim deal is much more favorable to the P5+1 than to Iran. It is the Iranians who should be feeling increasingly burdened by persistent sanctions and a continuing freeze on their nuclear program. Of course, the United States and its partners would like to make the current extension the last one. But if a sound agreement is not possible by the end of June, the option of another extension should not be ruled out. And if there is no agreement by June and the negotiations are discontinued, it should be Iran, and not the United States, that is responsible for pulling the plug.

Second, the United States should do whatever it can to maintain and enhance the effectiveness of existing sanctions. The Treasury Department should continue its aggressive efforts to remind governments and companies around the world that sanctions remain in place and that Iran "is not open for business." Undersecretary Cohen testified last week that, since the JPOA was signed, nearly 100 individuals and entities have been sanctioned for helping Iran evade sanctions and other offenses and that sanctions violators have received more than $350 million in penalties. U.S. officials should stress to their counterparts around the world that prospects for a peaceful, negotiated solution depend on not relaxing the pressure at this crucial stage of the negotiations.

Third, governments with access and influence in Tehran – especially those whose leaders are able to be in direct contact with Supreme Leader Khamenei – should be encouraged to impress on Iranian officials and especially the Supreme Leader that the international community expects Iran to take a realistic and flexible approach to the negotiations and that, if it fails to do so, Iran will only heighten concerns about the purpose of its nuclear program, will remain the target of economic sanctions, and will be unable to get its economy moving again.

Fourth, while negotiations are underway, the Administration should do contingency work with the Congress and its international partners on a Plan B – a plan for the eventuality that no agreement will be reached. Instead of confronting each other on the early enactment of a new sanctions law, the executive and legislative branches should begin now to jointly develop sanctions legislation that would be ready to be voted and immediately implemented in the event of a breakdown of the negotiations or an Iranian violation of the interim deal. The Administration should also begin now to consult key foreign partners on enhancements of the international sanctions regime as well as adjustments in cooperative defense plans that may be warranted in the wake of a breakdown of negotiations. At the same time, it should make clear, especially to Iranian audiences, that the United States remains fully committed to seeking a fair, negotiated solution to the nuclear issue and that work on Plan B is preparation for a contingency that hopefully will not arise. Presumably Iran is already working on a Plan B of its own.

Chairman ROYCE. I have got two questions, but one of Iran's paths to a bomb would be through its plutonium reactor at Arak. And indeed, in reading through some of your statements, Mr. Einhorn, you have referred to this reactor as a plutonium bomb factory.

As I recall, this was the issue that the French were so concerned about when that negotiation began, when it looked like we were going to into an interim agreement in November 2013. They raised the specter of this. And the administration insists that these negotiation will cut off all of Iran's paths to a bomb. But I was interested when I read the testimony of Ambassador Edelman, you say that the administration has relinquished its effort to shut off Iran's plutonium path to a bomb by converting its heavy water reactor at Arak.

And I was going to ask you what is the state of play here, Mr. Edelman?

Mr. EDELMAN. Well, I suspect that Bob has a better fix on what the exact state of play is than I do, but it is clear that the administration has retreated to a different standard which is to try and get the reactor rearranged, the core of the reactor rearranged in order to limit the production of plutonium rather than convert the reactor entirely.

Chairman ROYCE. Mr. Einhorn?

Mr. EINHORN. I have no doubt that the Arak reactor was designed in order to become a plutonium factory for nuclear weapons. I have no doubt about that.

But what has happened in the negotiations is that apparently Iran has agreed to redesign the reactor to reduce very, very substantially the amount of plutonium that is generated in the spent fuel. It was originally designed to operate on natural uranium which increases the weapons plutonium content of the spent fuel. They have apparently agreed to use enriched uranium fuel which greatly reduces the amount of plutonium produced annually to a level that makes it infeasible to try to break out using the plutonium route.

There are still disagreements. The U.S. would like to make this a lightwater reactor which makes it less reversible and the Iranians don't want to do that.

Chairman ROYCE. But they are not going to do that. They are going to reduce it, but not eliminate it.

Mr. EINHORN. No, you can't. Any reactor produces plutonium. The question is how much. And the way they have agreed to redesign it there are very low amounts.

Chairman ROYCE. They will reduce the amount. The other question I had was on the expiration date, or the sunset as it is called in the agreement. And last year, the committee heard testimony from a former State Department official who described the term ''comprehensive solution'' as a complete misnomer because according to the interim agreement, the restrictions put in place through such a comprehensive solution will only remain in place for a specific amount of time, so it can't be comprehensive. It is not permanent.

And as he pointed out, the comprehensive solution looked at that way is just an interim step itself. It is going to be an interim step, a temporary step. It is going to expire and after which Iran can engage on industrial scale enrichment. And it could then undertake activities that Holland, Japan, and Brazil are taking today.

So Mr. Einhorn, you had testified that a sound agreement would last about 15 years in your viewpoint. But Mr. Hannah notes that the sunset clause kicks in even if Iran is led in the future by the equivalent of an Ahmadinejad 2.0 or even if it is still the top sponsor of terrorism. So as Iran continues to reach to dominate the region, what is an acceptable length of time for an agreement? I will just ask the panel since this is simply going to be an interim agreement. And after that, it is going to be under their insistence, and of course, they are looking for a time frame, I guess, less than 10 years. But I will just tell you I remember the North Korean nuclear framework agreement. That doesn't seem that long ago and that was 20 years ago that we were talked into that. We see what the results were.

Mr. EINHORN. Mr. Chairman, in 2008, the P5+1 countries agreed that when Iran convinced the international community that its program was peaceful, then it would be able to pursue a program like any NPT party that is compliant. That was already in 2008.

I think the sunset provision frankly is unfortunate. I would like to have it a permanent agreement, but that is water under the bridge. But I think it is important to make it as long as possible and I say 15 years at a minimum.

Chairman ROYCE. Yes.

Mr. EINHORN. But it is important to recognize that even after 15 years, there will be very strong disincentives for Iran to go ahead and produce nuclear weapons. They would still face a very strong threat of not just economic sanctions, but military attack by the United States and its partners. So it is not as if they are swinging free and easy at that point. There would still be strong deterrent against them going that route.

Chairman ROYCE. Other members of the panel?

Mr. TAKEYH. I will just say briefly on this, there is nothing permanent about this particular concession. One of the things that I suggested that the administration can do is go back and say upon the expiration of the sunset clause, Iran will still have to go back to the U.N. Security Council as a sort of a probationary hearing and they can determine whether it can then proceed toward industrialization of the program and they can make that determination based on an entire range of factors such as other aspects of Iran's behavior. But I don't think this should be an eighth time type agreement.

Chairman ROYCE. Well, since the Supreme Leader says he wants 190,000 centrifuges, he is not thinking along the lines that you just articulated.

Mr. Hannah.

Mr. HANNAH. Mr. Chairman, I didn't agree with the decision in 2008, although that clearly didn't commit to any kind of deadline and time frame. The most I would have done is agree that we would have some kind of review committee at some point in time, perhaps after 15 years to look at and examine the question. But I think in the real world the absence of linkage between any kind of special inspection and verification regime and restrictions that we impose on Iran to divorce that from the basic heart and soul and nature of that regime and its war with the United States and Israel and our other allies in the regime, I just think it is folly, it is dangerous. And I think we will rue the day if we allow that to proceed.

I think I agree with Bob that this has been given away already by this administration and I don't think it can be reversed at this point in time without doing damage in the negotiations before you probably get a new administration in office.

Chairman ROYCE. So we will go to Ambassador Edelman. My point about the 190,000 centrifuges that the Supreme Leader says is his objective, that would be okay under this scheme. I mean if it goes 10 years after that, he is in a position to move forward with his goal, right?

Mr. EDELMAN. That is my understanding, Mr. Chairman. Like the other panelists, and I guess we are unanimous, all of us, I think, lament the fact that this is now a part of the negotiation. From my point of view, as a result of that, the only acceptable date that would be reasonable would be 20 years. But, partly because of the reasons that you just suggested in terms of the scope of ambition that the Supreme Leader has declared for the program.

I worry about the regional security implications of this going forward, because we will likely be leaving Iran as a threshold state. And that means all the other states in the region, notably including our allies, Israel, our Sunni Gulf Arab allies, are going to have to make a whole series of judgments about their security in a world where Iran is much closer to a nuclear weapon than it was in 2008, for instance. And I think that is going to have, as Mr. Hannah suggested, some very, very serious consequences for the region.

Chairman ROYCE. Thank you. Ambassador. Mr. Sherman.

Mr. SHERMAN. Let us not get carried away on one thing. Congress has agreed to nothing. No treaty has been submitted to this Congress for ratification. And in 2017, the Government of the United States is free to take whatever action it chooses at that time. Even if Congress were to pass a resolution in support of some agreement, not likely, that is binding only on that Congress.

If Iran wants a permanent agreement with the United States, let it agree to something good enough to gain ratification of the United States Senate as a treaty. And we have put the world on notice by publishing our Constitution, that something signed as a memo with one leader is perhaps morally binding on that leader.

Mr. Einhorn, your comments, I do want to mention first I think you have hit on the one best argument against Congress passing sanctions now. And that is the most influential American in the world, President Obama, has pretty much said that if Congress passes sanctions now that the rest of the world shouldn't follow and should regard us, the United States Government, as unreasonable. It may be a self-fulfilling prophecy. It may very well be that by announcing to the world that if Congress' acts were unreasonable, it ties our hands. I don't think it does, but it might.

You also, I think, well laid out the 1 year objective that we have in these negotiations, but keep in mind once the sanctions are lifted, Iran moves all of its foreign currency into Chinese banks, Cayman Island banks, tens of billions of dollars. And gets years of breathing room. After that, if they were to break out and we were to apply new sanctions, those sanctions wouldn't bite for a year. So the only possible action would be military action and I'm not sure this country would take military action. But remember, Iran gets to choose the time. So they can wait for the next Ukrainian crisis and then see whether the United States will take military action. Sanctions cannot go from zero to biting in 1 year, especially if foreign currency reserves have been moved.

Doctor, what is Iran's July 1 plan? Would they want a further extension and does that sell to the Iranian political powers? Are they ready with a breakout? What do they do on July 1, assuming they haven't signed an agreement with President Obama?

Mr. TAKEYH. I am not part of the Council, but it seems to me that they would be prepared for extension of the talks beyond that. For how long, I am not sure. Because increasingly, I think the regime will come under pressure from the Atomic Energy Organization and others for introducing new technologies that at this point are prohibited under the Joint Plan of Action. So at some point, the necessity of extending the talks and the necessity of technologically forging ahead of the program are likely to collide. So there is a time when Joint Plan of Action doesn't make sense for Iran's nuclear agencies who are planning to advance their program.

Mr. SHERMAN. And if they don't enter into an extension, and I realize they don't clue you in on this, but you are more clued in than I am, what do they do?

Mr. TAKEYH. I don't sit around and worry too much about the breakdown of negotiations that have thus far lasted 13 years. I think these negotiations go on in some way in some form.

Mr. SHERMAN. Thank you. I want to move on to Mr. Hannah. The question is what additional sanctions would actually bite? The most ideal and probably the one we are most likely to adopt is we take the Menendez-Kirk sanctions and we put them on a glide path all the way to zero. That is to say we turn to each country and with a glide path not lasting too long, you can't buy any Iranian oil and still use the U.S. banking system.

A second idea is that we fill the loophole in what we have already passed as far as government contracting and we declared all the major corporate conglomerates of the world that if you want even one—that all of your subsidiaries will have to abide by U.S. sanctions against Iran, not sell anything other than food and medicine, not buy any oil, if any of your subsidiaries won even one U.S. Government contract and we could further and make it state and local as well.

Other than that, does anybody on the panel have any ideas what should be in a sanctions bill?

Mr. HANNAH. I do think the oil one is critical, Congressman, because as you know, and I think as you stated, the world doesn't need Iranian oil any more. Eight years ago under the Bush administration, when we had serious problems with sanctions, there was a strong——

Mr. SHERMAN. I do have limited time. The chairman is indulging me a bit, but do you have anything on the list to add? I know how important that one item is. That is why I listed it first.

Mr. HANNAH. I think you could feasibly shut down transport going on, particularly shipping going in and out of Tehran. Ships that go into Tehran never get access to any American port. Possibly the same for air travel as well. Planes that go to Tehran get no access to American airports and American air space.

Mr. SHERMAN. Interesting idea. Anybody else have an idea to add to the list?

Mr. EDELMAN. I think, Mr. Sherman, you could add other sectors to the economy, construction. There are other things that we could do to make life even more difficult.

Mr. SHERMAN. Please provide a more thorough answer, all of you, for the record. Shall I try and sneak in one more question?

Chairman ROYCE. Sure.

Mr. SHERMAN. Okay, one more question. Let us say it is 15 years from now and Iran has not made extraordinary progress because we had such a great deal, but the deal is expired. They are signatory to not only the MPT, but the additional protocol. How quickly can they put together a stockpile of six weapons without being caught by the limited, intrusive investigations called for by the additional protocol? Does anybody have an answer?

Or more generally, is the additional protocol good enough by itself to prevent Iran from having a successful, covert nuclear program? Don't all answer at once.

Mr. Einhorn?

Mr. EINHORN. The additional protocol, I think, is kind of the gold standard now for the international inspections. It is not good enough certainly during an agreement for 15 or 20 years. I think it has to go well beyond. But I think it is important to remember one thing, that at least during the agreement, a covert program doesn't have one facility. It has maybe five or six different facilities. It takes 1 or 2 or 3 years to construct that covert program. So getting away with cheating at a covert location isn't so easy.

But there are elements that should continue beyond the expiration date as well. For example, the Iranians shouldn't be able to have a reprocessing plant. There are other kinds of things the administration should press on them to accept that go beyond the additional protocol.

Mr. SHERMAN. My time has expired.

Chairman ROYCE. We go to Ileana Ros-Lehtinen, chairwoman of the Middle East Subcommittee and long active in this issue of Iran sanctions.

Ms. ROS-LEHTINEN. Thank you very much, Mr. Chairman. As we heard this morning, the Senate has officially stated that no new sanctions legislation will be brought up for a vote until late March. And I think it is important to remember that the first sanctions that the U.S. began imposing against Iran were terrorism related. And that is being largely neglected as these ill-conceived, these secret and misguided nuclear negotiations continue to be extended for reasons passing understanding. In fact, as the negotiations continue, Iran support for terror has not waned, has actually increased.

Tehran calculates that President Obama is more willing to blame Congress for the talks failing than he is likely to blame this murderous and dangerous regime. So the result is that the Obama administration capitulates to Iran's demands and we get nothing, while Iran's dangerous actions continue to spread. And we need to look no further than the President's own so-called success story in Yemen.

Just a few days ago, the Iran-backed Houthi rebels arrested control of Yemen's capital and its government, giving Iran effective control over four Arab capitals. Yet, the administration carries on, alienating our allies, appeasing our enemies, even enlisting Iran as an asset. Just think about that.

In the battle against al-Qaeda in Yemen, and ISIL in Iraq and in Syria, these are situations for which Iran's terror proxies are responsible. And now the administration finds itself on the same side as Iran. Yet, all of this is off the table. It is not part of the nuclear negotiations. And the reality of the situation belies the President's narrative. The President threatens to veto Congress' attempt to hold Iran accountable, yet deadlines are repeatedly missed. Iran continues to impede the IAEA's verification efforts at every turn. And there are still many numerous other issues regarding the possible military dimension of Iran's nuclear weapons program.

Recently, it was reported that Iran, along with North Korea, is helping to build missile sites and a nuclear reactor in Syria, likely to outsource to enrichment capabilities to its proxy in Damascus, which would not be a violation of the JPOA. Iran continues its research and development of more advanced centrifuges, yet that also is not a violation, according to this administration. Iran is giving oil to Syria, not a violation. And it was announced that Iran, with the help of Russia, is actually building two new nuclear reactors and also somehow that is not a violation. And of course, Iran's continued progress on its ICBM program, its spread of terror, its support for terrorist groups, and its even-worsening human rights records, were never on the table for discussion to begin with.

So what exactly will the administration consider a violation? The implication for these nuclear negotiations are far reaching and we cannot be willing to carry on with this farce while Iran perfects its enrichment, its weaponization, its missile programs.

So to the panel, does any of this indicate that Iran is intent on actually reaching a nuclear agreement or is the regime use the guise of diplomacy to further its ambition including creating a nuclear weapon? And lastly, last week, Tony Blinken, as you saw in his testimony, confirmed what most of us already knew, that the administration's goal is not to prevent Iran from ever getting a nuclear weapon. It is merely to delay that action.

Even if we are successful in delaying nuclear capability for Iran to a year or 2, will that be enough to assuage other countries in the region like the Saudis, the Emiratis, from seeking their own nuclear capability? And do you believe that the administration will be willing to walk away from the negotiations if the status quo remains? To anyone who wishes to answer.

Ambassador.

Mr. EDELMAN. Ms. Ros-Lehtinen, it is very hard to quibble with your characterization of where we are. I would say on the question of whether—you were talking about Mr. Blinken saying that we are likely to have an extension.

Ms. ROS-LEHTINEN. Correct.

48

Mr. EDELMAN. I think that is the most likely outcome in part, because the answer to the first part of your question, "Has Iran made a strategic decision to forego a nuclear weapons program?" I think the answer is pretty clear. They have not. On the contrary, they feel that they have now successfully impressed upon the administration through the statements of the Supreme Leader, etcetera, that they must be allowed to have an industrial scale enrichment program at the end of this process. And so we have seen a demand of the international community that originally was a complete freeze on enrichment. Then we were going to have a couple of hundred, then a couple of thousand. Now we are talking about maybe as many as 9,000 centrifuges.

Ms. ROS-LEHTINEN. Nine thousand.

Mr. EDELMAN. Perhaps rearranged, perhaps unplugged, etcetera. We don't know yet what the outcome will be. The Iranians have 19,000 now. If you split the difference, you end up with about 9,000. And I think the answer to the question is no, they have not given up their desire and we have given up our objective of preventing them from having that capability. Instead, as we have discussed on this panel, looking at preventing them from breaking out or sneaking out within 1 year. That is where I am afraid we are.

To your question about how will others in the region see this, I think it is going to be very hard, particularly for a country say like the United Arab Emirates, which signed a 123 agreement with the United States to have its own nuclear power, completely foregoing any capability for enrichment, to look across the Gulf and see Iran allowed by agreement with the United States to have thousands of centrifuges, whatever the actual number ends up being and a capability to continue to enrich without calling into question the wisdom of their earlier agreement with the United States and the reliability of the United States, the guarantor of their security. And I think others in the region will make similar kinds of judgments.

Chairman ROYCE. Thank you, Ileana. Mr. Ted Deutch, ranking member of the Middle East Subcommittee. And I mentioned the horrendous human rights situation in Iran in my opening statement. I should add Mr. Deutch has long been active on behalf of his constituent, Mr. Levinson, and we would like to see a resolution to his case, as well as those of other Americans, including and imprisoned Washington Post reporter, and a former Marine, Amir Hekmati.

And on that note, I would ask unanimous consent to add a letter from the Hekmati family into the record. And Mr. Deutch is recognized.

Mr. DEUTCH. Thank you, Mr. Chairman, and thank you for making that point. Thank you for pointing out that as part of these talks while I know the fate of Bob Levinson, my constituent, and the others who are in Iran continues to be brought up, I think it is appropriate for us to have some expectation that as these talks continue, to see some good faith from the Iranians on these issues at least would be helpful to those of us who have concerns about the broader deal.

I want to start with a comment that I heard on one of the Sunday morning shows that if Congress—the suggestion was made that if Congress takes any sort of action at all, that Iran will be able to go to the world and say that the United States negotiated in bad faith. I would point out to all my colleagues here and to the administration something they know better than anyone, that it is inconceivable that anyone could make an argument that the United States is not negotiating in good faith when we entered into a JPOA which was extended once and which was extended again. And to suggest that Congress being involved in this process somehow suggests bad faith is just inaccurate and I think it is important for us to make that point. That is number one.

Number two. Just within the past few days, the IAEA director, speaking in Indonesia, said that in his address to the University of Indonesia, he said that "we are not in a position to provide credible assurance about the absence of undeclared nuclear material and activities in Iran, and therefore, to conclude that all nuclear material in Iran is in peaceful activities. In addressing the Iran nuclear issue, two things are important," he said. "First, with the cooperation of Iran, the agency needs to clarify issues with possible military dimensions to the satisfaction of member states. Also, Iran needs to implement the additional protocols so that the agency can provide credible assurance about the absence of undeclared nuclear material and activities in Iran."

The question I have is with everything on the table, Mr. Einhorn you said that it is in our interests that Congress shouldn't act, that it is in our interest to get another extension, that the Iranians are being hurt more. How is it that we shouldn't expect that at some point in this process in order for us to continue these talks we should require that Iran come clean on the possible military dimensions of their program and that they fully work with the IAEA to address their concerns? Why shouldn't that be something that we demand before we consider any other concessions going forward?

Mr. EINHORN. Thank you, Congressman. Let me just mention and actually clarify, I wasn't saying that I support another extension. What I was saying is, if necessary, we can afford it. We should push for an agreement as soon as we can get a sound agreement. But if that is not possible, because of Iranian intransigence, we can afford another extension because the current interim arrangement is in our interest, not in Iran's interest.

Mr. DEUTCH. Mr. Einhorn, I like your answer to the question, but I would, given what you just said, I would ask also if you could explain—and I understand the distinction that is made between the relief that is being provided and the money that is being held. But at some point, $700 million a month starts to really cut in to that $40 billion. And number two, as anyone perceives it, $700 million a month in concessions can't really be described as inconsequential.

Mr. EINHORN. Every month, the restricted accounts build up further, so they get deeper in the hole. Yes, they get $700 million a month back, but I think it is something like almost $2.5 billion that gets deposited in these restricted accounts that they can't get access to. So they are getting deeper into the hole. The $700 million doesn't mount up. What mounts up is the amount that they don't have access to.

Mr. DEUTCH. I would like you to address, if you could, perhaps after I am finished since I am running out of time, the PMD issue and maybe all of the members will be able to get back to it, but I would just conclude by pointing out that if there is a sense that it is okay to come up with a sanctions bill now that won't go into effect unless there is a breakdown in talks or unless Iran walks away, that that is exactly what this Congress has been trying to do all throughout, number one.

And number two, to those who are critical of the notion that we should increase pressure in order to have a stronger negotiating position with Iran, I would just ask that we stop debating the danger posed by the United States Congress and we refocus on the danger posed by a nuclear-armed Iran, one that would spark a nuclear arms race in the region, that would make Iran's proxies in Syria and Lebanon and Iraq and Yemen more dangerous, that would strengthen the terrorist groups that threaten the region and the world that Iran supports and controls. That is why some of us believe that since the IAEA isn't satisfied, we don't know about the military dimensions of the program. We don't know about what else may be happening inside Iran. And all the while, there may be penalties that Iran feels on the oil front, but it hasn't slowed them in their support of their terror proxies around the world. We need to call an end to this at some point.

Ms. ROS-LEHTINEN [presiding]. The gentleman's time has expired.

Mr. DEUTCH. Thank you.

Ms. ROS-LEHTINEN. Mr. Chabot of Ohio.

Mr. CHABOT. Thank you. I want to thank you, Madam Chairman, for calling this hearing and I want to echo the concerns that have already been expressed this morning about ongoing nuclear negotiations with Iran. I am afraid that if the Obama administration reaches a deal with a Iran, it is likely to be a really bad one because we have already conceded far beyond the parameters of what would be an acceptable agreement in my view.

Now just a couple of questions. Various reports indicate that negotiations remain deadlocked over fundamental issues such as the size of Iran's enrichment capability. At this point it is clear that Iran is stalling so that it can continue to absorb the $700 million per month in hard currency that it is receiving as a result of the sanctions relief. In order to change the current trajectory, I believe we need to increase the pressure on Iran because Iran does not believe it has much to lose from dragging on this negotiation process. That is my view.

Why should we have any confidence in the administration's negotiations with Iran? Isn't it reasonable to conclude that Iran is benefitting from the sanctions as I stated, the relief, pocketing the $700 million per month in hard currency and just stringing the U.S. along as long as possible, and in the end, we are either going to end up with no deal or a lousy one? Mr. Edelman?

Mr. EDELMAN. Well, as I said in my statement, Mr. Chabot, I am also very worried about the trajectory of this negotiation. I think if you look back, again, as far back as 2003, what one sees is the international community's red line amounting to kind of a serial concession to Iranian intransigence. So for instance, in the 2003–2005 period, there was a freeze on enrichment activity and the Iranians, the then nuclear negotiator for Iran, subsequently explained in a book saying it was a tactic that the Iranians used in order to work out some of the difficulties, the technical difficulties they were having in their program. That Iranian nuclear negotiator is now the President of Iran, President Rouhani.

So I think not only does one have to worry about the current state of the negotiations, but really the whole history here has been one of Iranian intransigence leading to further concessions. And if you are sitting in Tehran assessing this, the conclusion you would draw from this is the longer you hold out, the more extensions you get in the negotiations, the more concessions you are likely to win.

Mr. CHABOT. Thank you. Mr. Takeyh, let me turn to you. I am already down to only 2 minutes left. You said we should listen to what they say, and I tend to agree with you on that. We had the previous leader say that he wanted to wipe Israel off the map. We have the current leader who still chants ''Death to America.'' Iran has said quite clearly on a number of occasions that they are determined to have a nuclear industrial program. Why should we have any confidence that negotiations with these people will end well?

Mr. TAKEYH. I would say the way the negotiating strategy has taken place, paradoxically, it makes an impasse more likely. Every time, as I think Eric said, we have met Iranian intransigence, we have adjusted our red lines. For Iranians to accept our current set of concessions means they would have to forego a future set of concessions. As a result, there is sort of a impasse built into these talks.

The policy in the summer of 2012, as Bob knows, was stop, ship, shot. That clearly is not the policy today and that clearly was an aspect of the Joint Plan of Action. So as the red line has moved, and it has moved frankly for a decade across administrations, Israeli red lines have moved. The Iranian strategy of being patient and has a measure of forbearance has yielded, unfortunately, nuclear concessions.

Mr. CHABOT. I am almost out of time. Mr. Einhorn?

Mr. EINHORN. Congressman, you mentioned that Iran would simply pocket $700 million a month. Let me just point out that for every month they lose about $2.14 billion worth of oil revenues, about $15 billion over the next 6 months and that they are going to take a hit because of the reduction in the price of oil. As time goes on, they get deeper in the hole.

Mr. CHABOT. I am almost out of time. Let me just conclude by saying that my concern is that the Obama administration is so desperate for a deal that Israel and our allies in the region and ultimately the United States itself, our security is in jeopardy. And that is why I am so disappointed, concerned, and this has been a disaster as far as I am concerned. I yield back.

Ms. ROS-LEHTINEN. Thank you, Mr. Chabot. Ms. kelly of Illinois.

Ms. KELLY. Thank you, Madam Chair. For years, Iran used a secret facility at Fordow, built into the side of a mountain to advance their nuclear program. We know Iran has the history with the covert program. A potential deal with Iran rests on our assumption that Iran is not continuing an overt nuclear program. What steps need to be taken to ensure that they are not racing toward a bomb at a covert facility?

Mr. HANNAH. Thank you, Congresswoman. I would just say that in terms of what my testimony was about and trying to stiffen the administration's position to mitigate the risk that I think we run of the kind of the deal that we are heading towards, I think we really need to pay attention to the verification and inspection regime. I think the IAEA additional protocol is not sufficient. I do believe we need a special inspection and verification regime for Iran. I think the Congress should insist on that. If it could it put in a joint resolution, I think it would be fantastic. But it essentially has to be what South Africa did when it gave up its nuclear weapons: Evidence that it had truly made a strategic decision to give up its nuclear weapons and agree to inspections that would be as close to the ideal as possible of any time, anywhere, anyone you want to interview you get access to. And I think that would be a very good barometer of whether or not the Iranians have, in fact, made a strategic choice to give up their ambition to have nuclear weapons.

Ms. KELLY. Thank you.

Mr. EDELMAN. Ms. Kelly, if I could just add to my colleague's comment, several members have raised the issue of the past military dimensions of the Iranian program. And I think it is absolutely incumbent on the administration to make sure that the IAEA gets satisfaction on this before we reach a final agreement because, for the life of me, I don't understand how one would begin to design the kind of inspection regime that John was just talking about until we have gotten to the bottom of all of the suspected military dimensions of the Iranian program.

Mr. TAKEYH. I will just say one thing before yielding to Bob. There is a lot of discussion about the type of inspection regime that should accompany an agreement. IAEA does not have satisfactory access to Iranian nuclear facilities today, as acknowledged by IAEA reports. There has been a work plan negotiated between IAEA and Iran that remains incomplete. The first work plan was negotiated in 2006, 9 years ago. So at the very least the negotiators should demand that IAEA complete the work plan and Iran give access today, not as a component of a prospective agreement.

Mr. EINHORN. Can I say that I agree with John that the additional protocol is not enough. We have to have what I call additional protocol plus. We have to have much greater access. We have to have access to military installations. The Iranians are resisting this. We have to insist on the ability to go to military installations.

The IAEA has to be satisfied with Iran's record of the past, these possible military dimensions. I don't think it is going to be possible to learn everything about the past, but we need to insist on knowing enough about the past so we are confident that those activities are not continuing in the present and will not continue in the future.

Ms. KELLY. How will we know what enough is? What will be that measure to know what enough is?

Mr. EINHORN. Well, it is a combination of what we hear from them about the past, plus what we are prepared to—what they are prepared to agree to in terms of intrusive measures going forward. I think the combination of the two would hopefully give us the confidence that they don't have a covert program.

Ms. KELLY. Any other comments? Thank you. I yield back.

Mr. CONNOLLY. Would my colleague yield?

Ms. KELLY. Yes.

Mr. CONNOLLY. Thank you. Thank you. Mr. Hannah, I really am struck with your suggestion because it just seems to me Congress is once again probably going down a rather feckless road. It makes us feel good. It allows us to pound our chest and prove our bona fides, but it is not efficacious. The idea of an inspection regime modeled after, for example, South Africa, that kind of agreement is to me a very helpful thing for you to suggest. So that is definitely something I think we ought to be exploring frankly before we start going down the road of additional sanctions which could only probably probably queer the deal. And I don't think Congress wants to take responsibility for queering the deal. Do you want to comment?

Mr. HANNAH. Thank you, Congressman. On South Africa, I think it is also worthwhile knowing that despite the fact that South Africa up front made that admission and made that agreement to that kind of inspection regime incredibly intrusive, according to Olli Heinonen, the former IAEA deputy director for inspections in Iran, that took 17 years to verify everything that South Africa had and to make sure we had a full understanding of the South African program. Here, we are talking about at best, at best, 15 years for a regime that is still engaged in a lie that goes to the hear of what this negotiation is all about, that they continue to maintain that they have never had any kind of ambition to have nuclear weapons which will be——

Mr. POE [presiding]. The gentlelady's time has expired. The Chair will recognize the gentleman from South Carolina, Mr. Wilson, for 5 minutes.

Mr. WILSON. Thank you, Judge Poe. And thank each of you for being here today. I think it has been very helpful. And Ambassador Edelman, your concerns about the course of negotiations with your background, this is really important for the American people to know.

Additionally, to me, it is really unfortunate that this administration did not give, I believe, sufficient encouragement to the young people of Iran who years ago, just a few years ago, were seeking to rebuild a modern, advanced nation. We could have given encouragement. I will never forget the young accountant who bled to death as she was laying on the street. The people of Iran want better. And we need to be encouraging them.

In regard to that, Mr. Hannah, what is your analysis of the logic to the President's negotiating strategy that the threat of stronger sanctions will drive the Iranians away, rather than compel them to make a better and real agreement? It seems illogical to me and many of my constituents in the reverse of reality.

Mr. HANNAH. I think it is unfortunate that the President, the way he has approached the issue of prospective sanctions. I think he is essentially bought into an Iranian narrative and I think up front in advance he is essentially granting legitimacy if Iran decides to act on prospective sanctions and walk away from this deal. They have essentially got the President of the United States more or less saying they would be justified in doing that, that he has been much tougher on the Congress than he has been on Iran in these talks. And I think the focus of sanctions, I don't believe it would lead Iran to walk away from these negotiations. If it did it would be only temporary. I think pressure is the only thing that has worked with the Iranian regime and I think pressure is our best means of getting a diplomatic settlement in this situation and actually avoiding war. Quite the contrary to what the President suggests.

Mr. WILSON. Avoiding war and threat to America, our allies.

Dr. Takeyh, Iran for decades has sponsored numerous terrorist attacks in places as far flung as Thailand, Beirut, New Delhi, Lagos, Nairobi, including the 2011 plot to assassinate the Saudi Arabian Ambassador to the United States and bomb the Israeli and Saudi Embassies in Washington. How can the United States trust such a government to keep any agreement? This is in the context of demonstrators in Tehran carrying signs in English proclaiming ''Death to America. Death to Israel.''

Mr. TAKEYH. I think that is a fair point. I would suggest that in Islamic republics' conception, international law and international norms are conspiracies, forged by the Western powers and inflicted upon it in an unfair and injudicious way. It is kind of difficult to suggest that Iran can be a member of the NPT in good standing while at the same time being a leading sponsor of terrorism. The two states cannot be cojoined in a sort of a logical construct. That is why I think once there is an agreement, the immediate challenge of it is detection of inevitable Iranian violations. And I am not quite sure how in the aftermath of an agreement you can deal with those violations in a sort of a systematic way with re-instructional sanctions and penalties because I think the inclination would be to have an American delegation meet an Iranian delegation and highlight those disagreements and those violations and presumably they take some corrective action. But I suspect if Iran does not violate its arms control agreement prospectively, it is the first time in history it has not violated international legal instrument.

Mr. WILSON. That is incredible. Thank you. Additionally, the American people need to know as Iran is claiming or the regime, that this is for peaceful purposes, they are also, Mr. Einhorn, developing a ballistic missile capability. Already they have a capability of striking as far as Southeastern Europe, Greece, Bulgaria, Romania. And they are developing a greater ICBM. They have launched a satellite. In light of that, with this delivery system, should the long-term agreement include limitations on a ballistic missile capability?

Mr. EINHORN. I think it would be good if there could be ballistic missile constraints in a nuclear deal. I don't think it is going to happen. The Iranians say that their missiles are for conventional weapons delivery, not for nuclear, so this has no part to play. I think we are going to have to pursue quite aggressively the question of Iranian ballistic missile capability, but separately from these negotiations. I think it is very important. I think the administration tries very hard to interdict procurement by Iran of equipment and technology for Iran's missile program. I think this should be a top priority. The ballistic missile defense programs we have we are working on with our European partners are designed to counter Iran's ballistic missile capability. But I think making it a part of the nuclear negotiations is going to be hard.

Mr. TAKEYH. I will just add one thing.

Mr. POE. The gentleman's time has expired. The gentleman's time has expired. Thank you. The Chair recognizes one of our new members from Pennsylvania, Mr. Boyle, for 5 minutes.

Mr. BOYLE. Well, thank you, Mr. Chairman. It is an honor to be on such an important committee. I am someone who is generally a supporter of the President and this administration. That having been said, I have a difficult time understanding the logic that if Congress were to act and say not sanctions today, but sanctions by a date certain if negotiations were to fail, that somehow that is unreasonable or somehow then we would be responsible for sinking these negotiations. When we were up against the November 24th deadline, and then we decided and agreed to yet another round of overtime to push things another 7 months, I think many reasonable people, who even might not have been supporters of sanctions at that time, came over to the view that clearly we cannot allow negotiations to go on indefinitely.

George Mitchell, who successfully negotiated the Good Friday agreement in Belfast, talked about the importance of having a deadline for those negotiations because there were some issues that have been debated for hundreds of years and could go on being debated for centuries to come.

So I have to say before I get to my question, I really disagree with the view that if Congress were to act and make clear what sanctions would be in the event these negotiations fail, I disagree that that would somehow be irresponsible.

Now getting to the possibility of a deal, knowing that Rouhani is not the ultimate decider, he is not the great leader. That said, there does seem to be somewhat of a moderating force in Iran that is more concerned with ending the sanction regime and being an economic power rather than going down the military path.

How much of a percentage of the Iranian regime do you think that represents? And frankly, how emboldened would they be even if there were a deal that they wanted to accept? What authority or power would they really have ultimately to be able to agree to that?

Mr. TAKEYH. On the ballistic missile issue, the U.N. Resolution 1625 has that which was negotiated in May 2010. I think there is one difference between President Rouhani and the office of the Supreme Leader. President Rouhani seems to recognize that Iran's economic situation is unlikely to improve without an arms control agreement. That particular logic is not obvious to the office of the Supreme Leader. But I would answer that by saying so what? So what does President Rouhani's recognition of that fact mean, given the fact that unlike President Ahmadinejad is not willing to buck the system? He is likely to remain within the parameters and red lines that are negotiated between his office and those of the Supreme Leader.

So irrespective of that agreement, which I think there is some indication that there is, it is a disagreement without significant consequence.

Mr. BOYLE. Does anyone else have a comment on that? Well, before I yield back, I would just say something that I believe my colleague, Congressman Sherman said at the very beginning of these hearings. To the extent that we can do anything with hard power, but also with soft power to embolden moderating forces and modernizing forces in Iran, it is certainly in our interest and certainly seems there can be far more to do than what we have been doing.

Do you have a comment?

Mr. HANNAH. Thank you, Congressman. Can I just ask the chair first if I could have entered into the record a new FDD Report, "Foundation for Defense and Democracy, The Case for Deadline Triggered Sanctions on Iran?"

Mr. POE. Without objection, the document will be entered into the record.

Mr. HANNAH. Thank you, sir. What I would say, Congressman, is we have had this debate over time in the past with the Congress consistently saying that we need more leverage, we need more sanctions in order to get Iran to have any possibility of getting a deal with the Iranians. And consistently administrations have argued to the Congress that, in fact, no that really won't be helpful. They go too far. You will alienate our international partners and you will empower radicals inside of Iran who want to keep pushing that nuclear program forward.

I would say we had a definitive answer to that argument when Congress finally went ahead and got the administration to agree to those crippling sanctions in 2012. By the time those went into effect in the middle of 2012, within a year, not only had the entire Iranian political system thrown upside down and the Supreme Leader allowing a more moderate, pragmatic face like Hassan Rouhani to come into power, but you also had Hassan Rouhani racing as fast as he could back to the negotiating table to try and halt the continued escalation of U.S. sanctions which was happening at that time. That, to me, is pretty good evidence that I think on these issues, Congress' judgment has been pretty good historically.

Mr. POE. The gentleman's time has expired. The Chair recognizes himself for 5 minutes. Thank you, gentlemen, for being here.

In the State of the Union address, the President said this:

> "Our diplomacy is at work with respect to Iran, where for the first time in a decade we have halted the progress of its nuclear program and reduced its stockpile of nuclear material."

That statement earned the President three Pinocchios from the Washington Post. It is not true. It is either a mistake or it is a falsehood. It seems to me that the United States and Western Europe in dealing with Iran and expecting some deal where we continue to back off sanctions, we are nothing more than gullible and playing the chamberlain on this issue. It seems to me that this hug diplomacy with Iran is like the West being the timid sheep and if we lay down with the jackal of the desert, we will become the mutton meal of the jackal.

I want to ask you specifically about the statement of the President. Mr. Takeyh, would you like to comment on that statement?

Mr. TAKEYH. I will yield to Bob in a minute. I do think the Joint Plan of Action has imposed some interim restraints on various aspects of the Iranian program such as production of medium-range fuel and 20 percent and the installation of new centrifuges. And it hasn't addressed some other issues such as research and development which I think is particularly glaring.

Now under the Joint Plan of Action, Iran had to maintain a threshold of w enriched uranium to some degree. Bob will know the number for sure. I think somehow they have gone above that at times. But I do think it has exercised some interim steps and restraints into the Iranian program.

Mr. POE. I have more questions and if we have time we will come back for the comments. I am glad you all are excited about answering these questions.

Mr. Takeyh, you said that the Iranians have never—is that right, did you say they have never agreed or fulfilled an international agreement in the past? Is that what you said?

Mr. TAKEYH. I think it is the genetic propensity of the system to regard international law as an unfair imposition resulting from Western conspiracy.

Mr. POE. Have they ever agreed to an agreement?

Mr. TAKEYH. Compliance is always tentative.

Mr. POE. Compliance. So they have never complied?

Mr. TAKEYH. Compliance is always tentative.

Mr. POE. Tentative. All right. It seems to me that the policy of the Iran Government is reflected in the Supreme Leader's statement that it is the goal of Iran to destroy the United States and Israel in reverse order, Israel first, then the United States.

As far as you know, has that policy, that foreign policy, changed? Ambassador.

Mr. EDELMAN. Well, I defer to Ray who is more expert than I on Iran. But I think Iranian foreign policy has been from a strategic point of view rather consistent since the revolution in 1979. There have been lots of tactical shifts and moves back and forth, but the overall objective of the revolution's foreign policy I think has been consistent.

Mr. POE. Mr. Hannah?

Mr. HANNAH. I think the answer is no. It hasn't changed and if you do actually listen to their words and believe what they say, they are telling you every week some senior political or military leader in that regime is telling you that their objectives of world without America and destroying the State of Israel is still very much in place.

Mr. POE. So that is their goal. Does the United States policy deal with that issue? Are we hoping to change their mind or are we hoping to force them to change their mind? What is our policy toward the comment that they want to eliminate us? All right, Mr. Einhorn, you have been wanting to answer a question. This one is yours.

Mr. EINHORN. Okay. It is the policy to counter Iran's destabilizing behavior wherever it is and to beef up the defenses of our partners in the region so that they can withstand intimidation and pressure from the Iranians.

Mr. POE. Let me interrupt you there. If the Iranians get nuclear weapons, don't you think that there will be a rush with Saudi Arabia, Turkey, and Egypt to get nuclear weapon programs, Mr. Takeyh?

Mr. TAKEYH. I do think there will be an inclination to move toward appropriation of such technologies. And that is something for the United States to be very mindful of proliferation. I do think at times we tend to have exaggerated views of cascades and so forth, namely that one nuclear power can trigger similar things. And that would be a very great challenge for the United States to tem- per——

Mr. POE. Do you think those three countries will be encouraged by the fact that Iran gets nuclear weapons to have their own nuclear weapon program?

Mr. TAKEYH. I think they are already encouraged to move in the direction of indigenous enrichment which is a precursor to such weaponry.

Mr. POE. My time has expired. The Chair will recognize the gentleman from Rhode Island, Mr. Cicilline, for 5 minutes.

Mr. CICILLINE. Thank you, Mr. Chairman. Thank you to the witnesses for being here today to discuss this incredibly important issue. I, for one, am grateful to the administration for their efforts to bring the Iranian Government to the table for these historic negotiations. I think it is important that we remember exactly what we are talking about here if the negotiations were to fall apart. At the moment, the administration is attempting to reach a diplomatic solution to prevent Iran from acquiring a nuclear weapon. Should these negotiations fail, the United States, the international community together must be prepared to respond appropriately including by using force, if necessary. But I think it is absolutely vital that we undertake in good faith every reasonable effort that we can to reach a non-military solution and devote all the time and energy necessary to do that.

The President has asked Congress to give him until the end of June to reach a deal and I, for one, am inclined to honor that request. However, we all agree that Iran has to understand this process will not be open ended or indefinite.

And with that, I go to my first question. The administration has said that the Iranian economy has been crippled by the sanctions. A recent State Department fact sheet said that Iran's economy contracted nearly 7 percent in the last year and contracted a further 3.4 percent through December 2013. Yet, we have also seen recent economic analysis that says that the Iranian economy is beginning to recover as a result of the sanctions relief under the Joint Plan of Action. Who is right? What has the impact been of the limited sanction relief that we have already provided? Are the sanctions still providing for us the kind of leverage that we need at the negotiating table to get the right deal? And what has been the impact of the drop in oil prices on the Iranian economy? And I invite whoever has the best and most accurate information with respect to this issue.

Mr. TAKEYH. I would just say they are both right. The State Department Fact Sheet that captured the situation in 2013 is correct and the IMF report that has suggested incremental growth in the Iranian economy since then is also correct.

Mr. EINHORN. Congressman, I think what has happened is a kind of Rouhani effect. Rouhani's economic managers are much more competent than Ahmadinejad's economic managers. And so you have had some incremental improvements. But I think especially with the oil price drop and the continuation of our sanctions, the Iranian economy cannot possibly recover. I think sensible Iranians understand that. There has been a huge drop in per capita GDP. The rial, their currency, has dropped something like 56 percent from earlier years and even something like 19 percent from November 2013. I think the data indicates that their economy is in really bad shape. Treasury Secretary Jack Lew said it is like they are at the bottom, they are stagnating at the bottom of a recession. And I think that is the reality.

Mr. HANNAH. Congressman, if I can, I would just say that whatever Bob says might be true, but I have no doubt that the IMF is right despite all of the—and they are in deep trouble economically. The trendline and trajectory is slowly upward, a reduction of economic pressure from where it was when the JPAO was signed. And I would just say that we have no historical experience of successfully denuclearizing its state when the economic, political, and military pressures are all going in the wrong direction, that is, decreasing, rather than intensifying.

Mr. CICILLINE. My second question is that some observers have suggested to us that Iran, the political leadership in Iran, the Supreme Leader, and the Iranian people, as a result of their efforts, have been convinced that somehow a nuclear weapons capability is either essential to their national identity or essential to their self defense. If that is true that they successfully persuaded themselves and the Iranian people of that, does that make a final deal on this impossible? Because in the end if they conclude, however erroneous it is, that it is essential for their self defense and they have convinced the Iranian people of that and in the context of Rouhani sort of running on some effort to change this sanctions regime, does it make both a deal impossible because a deal can obviously not include their ability to have nuclear weapons? And secondly, does it make the collapse of negotiations inevitable and a replacement of Rouhani by someone who is more hard line. And I will start with you, Mr. Einhorn.

Mr. EINHORN. Congressman, Iran's leaders have convinced the Iranian public that their enrichment capability is almost a national birthright, a source of dignity and so forth. I think there is a consensus across the political spectrum. They are not prepared to give up enrichment.

They haven't convinced the Iranian people that nuclear weapons are essential. Quite the opposite. The Supreme Leader says there is a religious decree of fatwa against nuclear weapons which is a good thing. Whether or not it is honest, it is a good thing because in the Iranian public they have the impression that this is not the policy of their country

Mr. HANNAH. Congressman, I would just note that I think it is going to be very difficult to get a deal. I don't think it is impossible, but I think you really have to be able to present the regime with a choice that either they are going to continue with this program or their regime is going to be held at real serious risk of either economic collapse or military attack. I think the Congress had put the administration in a position where that kind of choice was coming true for the Iranians in the fall of 2013. And I now worry that that is not necessarily the choice they are facing any more.

Mr. CICILLINE. Thank you. I yield back, Mr. Chairman.

Chairman ROYCE [presiding]. Thank you, Mr. Cicilline. We go to Mr. Ted Yoho of Florida.

Mr. YOHO. Thank you, Mr. Chairman. Thank you, gentlemen. Take me back and kind of a review for maybe the new people and myself of why we started the negotiations? Who started it? Did we initiate it or did Iran come to the table and say we want to negotiate? Just real briefly any of you.

Mr. EDELMAN. Congressman, I think I said in my statement we have had about 10 years' worth of diplomacy. So this really goes back to 2003 when the EU–3 was negotiating with Iran over the early stages of its enrichment program after it was exposed by the national——

Mr. YOHO. What I mean, if I can cut you off, what I mean is with the negotiation and the release of the sanctions here recently, the current ones.

Mr. EDELMAN. The Joint Plan of Action?

Mr. YOHO. Right.

Mr. EDELMAN. That was undertaken after the election of President Rouhani.

Mr. YOHO. Did they come to us or did we say hey, let us start negotiating on this and straighten this out?

Mr. EDELMAN. I think it would be fair to say that the administration since President Obama came in had been reaching out to Iran in the hope that they could engage them in a negotiation. It became possible after Rouhani was elected.

Mr. YOHO. Mr. Hannah, what did we get out of the negotiation? What was the benefit for us out of this?

Mr. HANNAH. I think as Mr. Einhorn has explained that the JPAO does commit Iran to certain tactical pauses in certain elements of its current nuclear program. It happens to be on the enrichment end that they were pausing elements of the program that they have already quite perfected, that they don't really need to improve in order to race forward to a nuclear weapon.

Mr. YOHO. And that is something I want to bring out because if you look over the past 25, 30 years, they have been progressing this way as an isolated state for the most part with sanctions on or off. And I see them progressing to this point. And I don't see that we got really a whole lot out of beginning these negotiations.

Let me ask you, 10 years from now do you see a nuclear armed Iran? Mr.—how do you pronounce your name?

Mr. TAKEYH. I got the easy one. Ten years from now will Iran have nuclear weapons? I am not sure I can answer that question, Congressman, with any degree of precision.

Mr. YOHO. Let me tell you what I have heard over the last 2 years, my first term in Congress. We have had all kinds of experts sitting right where you are and they said within 6 months and this was going back to 2013, that within 6 months Iran would have enough nuclear materials within 6 months to have five or six weapons. So I can only assume these experts, some of you guys might have been on that panel, you know, they were correct. So I can assume at this point, listening to the experts that Iran has the capability of that.

In addition, we know they have detonated a trigger device. They have their ICBM missiles. So I will get to where I want to go on this. But when I was in vet school, I had a professor, things were real simple for us. He said if it looks like a duck, walks like a duck, smells and quacks like a duck, it is probably a duck.

What I see with the intent of Iran is the same thing. With the rhetoric coming out, the extinction of Israel, the death of the Great Satan, the Little Satan, Israel, one bomb nation, the end of Zionism and all the other rhetoric that comes out of there, I have to believe what they say is they don't mean to carry on just a nuclear power program, that they are intent on getting a nuclear weapon, if so, and I really believe they are hell bent on doing that. What are we doing? Because what I see is this is an exercise in futility, especially with the sunset clause.

Regardless of what we negotiate within 5, 10 years or whatever that date is, all restrictions are gone, so therefore they are going to be that. You know, to answer my own question, I see them either having it, the capability, or already having it. What are we doing as a nation to protect when that point comes? What are we doing to prepare for that next phase?

Mr. TAKEYH. I would say one thing in point of agreement with you, it is at times suggested that Iran will have all the ingredients of nuclear weapons, but not cross the line. I think if they get there, they will cross.

Now what are we doing in the region? I think at this point if there is an agreement, I suspect that any administration in power will try to enhance the security of the regional allies to various deployments and various anti-missile forces and so on.

Mr. YOHO. Mr. Einhorn, and then I want to add one more comment at the end.

Mr. EINHORN. The U.S. intelligence community has decided year after year after year that Iran is insisting on preserving an option the Supreme Leader wrote, but it has made no decision yet on whether actually to build nuclear weapons. I think this is an issue for the future. What we can do through an agreement is to deter them from making that decision to cross the line. We can do it by making the path ahead to nuclear weapons very long, long breakout time, getting the capability to detect breakout at a very early stage and also threatening them with consequences if we detect breakout, so that they know that they will not be able to succeed. I think that is the theory of the case.

Mr. YOHO. Thank you. And I yield back.

Chairman ROYCE. Thank you. We go to Mr. Alan Lowenthal of California.

Mr. LOWENTHAL. Did I go out of order here?

Chairman ROYCE. Yes, I missed Mr. Gerry Connolly. I best go by seniority. Mr. Connolly, Virginia.

Mr. CONNOLLY. Thank you, Mr. Chairman. Thank you, Mr. Lowenthal. Welcome to the panel.

Mr. Hannah, if I heard you correctly, you basically said and I don't want to put—but what I heard you say to us was it is worth the gamble if the past is prologue, sanctions didn't drive them away. In fact, sanctions helped bring them to the table. What probability though would you put on that not working this time, that unintentionally—we have got to remember Iran also was a political system and there are factions. And there is probably a faction that would like to resolve this issue more in our favor than not and then there is another faction, probably the Supreme Leader leads that faction that is very suspicious of this and frankly wants to see the status and everything else that flows from becoming a nuclear power.

We need to be careful that we are not unwittingly playing to a faction not in our interest, not that we have friendly factions, but less friendly factions. Don't we need to be a little bit careful about new sanctions and the risk that the fact the Iranians walk away from the table and use it as an excuse to say we are done. And then the only option is what a previous panelist referred to as kinetic options.

Mr. HANNAH. Thank you, Congressman. I do think that you have to, however low the probability you place on it, you have to hold out the contingency that perhaps the President is right and that Iran will try and use this as a chance to break out and resume its nuclear program. I think it is unfortunate that it might be part of a self-fulfilling prophecy and that I think the President is now giving the Iranians, as well as some of our international partners, the grounds and the arguments to do exactly that. The President didn't have to do that. I can think of a much different approach he would have taken in which he would have said I don't agree with the Congress, I don't think I need this power. I don't think it is in violation of the letter of the JPOA. We have got enough waivers in these prospective sanctions that if necessary I will continue to prevent sanctions from going into place on the Iranians, but still make the argument that if the Iranians made the fateful choice to try and break out, this Congress and this Executive Branch would be completely unified in mobilizing our international partners to say that would be outrageous, and that if Iran wanted to play that dangerous game, there is a much higher, higher price to pay for them potentially beyond whatever is being considered in these new prospective sanctions. But I do think you have to take it into account and plan for it that that could be an outside possibility.

Mr. CONNOLLY. Ambassador Edelman.

Mr. EDELMAN. Mr. Connolly, if I could add to Mr. Hannah's answer. I, from my own experience in government, am somewhat skeptical of arguments about sanctions driving people away from the negotiating table. During the course of the six party talks with North Korea in the Bush administration in 2007, we were told unless the Banco Delta Asia sanctions were lifted, North Korea was going to walk away from the table. We lifted those sanctions.

We then took North Korea off the terrorism list in the summer of 2008. We then got them out from under the restrictions of the Trading With the Enemy Act and those negotiations collapsed and failed anyway, despite the relief of sanctions. I think that was because North Korea had not made a fundamental decision to limit its nuclear weapons program and give it up and I think that is the same issue we are facing now with Iran.

Mr. CONNOLLY. I am going to ask the chair if he will indulge the other two panelists to answer the same question.

Chairman ROYCE. Proceed.

Mr. CONNOLLY. I thank the chair. I do want to say to you, Ambassador Edelman, I take your point. But what if you are wrong? It is a rhetorical question. But I mean as a member who has to vote I would hope every one of us takes that responsibility seriously.

Mr. EDELMAN. And you should.

Mr. CONNOLLY. When Congress queers the deal in foreign policy it is a big deal. The League of Nations comes to mind. I am not sure that was our finest moment. And so we have got to tread carefully. We can't just be facile about this, not that you are being, but we must weigh this very carefully and we do have to ask the question what if we are wrong?

May I ask the other two panelists, if either one wanted to answer the question? And I thank the chair for his indulgence.

Mr. TAKEYH. I think there are a number of reasons why Iran has remained on the table that have nothing to do with the nuclear issue. Number one is it seeks legitimization of its nuclear program. That can only come at the table. Number two, it does get a measure of economic relief, not in terms of the $700 million, but in terms of the atmosphere that is conducive to economic growth. That would also evaporate if it leaves the table.

Finally, Iran's very aggressive policies in the region are not being really challenged by the United States partly because of the nuclear negotiations so that veneer of protection will move. So there are a lot of reasons why Iranians have an interest in the table, in the negotiations, even if those negotiations are impassed.

Mr. EINHORN. Congressman, no one knows for sure whether new sanctions legislation will scuttle the deal. By the way, all of the P5+1 partners, all of whom have Embassies in Tehran and have good contacts with the Iranians, all of them believe that it would be very dangerous for us to pursue this course and it could well undermine the negotiations. But we just don't know. I tend to believe, I tend to agree with Eric, I tend to believe they won't walk out, but I think it could have a deleterious effect on the prospect for greater Iranian flexibility. The question is are they necessary? Is it worth the risk? Should we take that risk? Because right now we have strong economic sanctions in place that are continuing to hurt the Iranians. We have the oil price drop which is also hurting the Iranians.

And we can always come back. If we need to in June, we can come back quickly and we can legislate new sanctions at that point. And I suggested in my statement earlier, the Executive and the Legislative Branches should be working now on new sanctions legislation. Work them out. Get agreement. Work together and have something that can be voted on quickly and implemented quickly, if necessary, at the end of June or whenever. So I think that is the question congressmen have to ask themselves, is it worth the risk?

Mr. TAKEYH. Can I just say one thing about a conversation that you and I had, Congressman Connolly, at this hearing and when I said to you that the administration has to come back and say why does it think at the time of the last extension the next 6 months will be different than the last 6 months? You and I had that conversation.

It turned out the last 6 months were not that different from the previous one. Whatever your view on sanctions is, the administration is obligated to come to this House and say why do they think the next 6 months will be different than the last 6 months? Why do they think they have sufficient coercive leverage in the negotiations that are admittedly stalemated?

Mr. CONNOLLY. And Mr. Chairman, picking up on that——

Mr. PERRY [presiding]. Will the gentleman suspend? I appreciate your time, but you have got to let folks weigh in. The gentleman's time has expired. The Chair recognizes Mr. Zeldin.

Mr. ZELDIN. Thank you, Chairman. I want to thank Chairman Ed Royce and the Foreign Affairs Committee for taking a leadership role on this issue. Regardless of whether the President is getting played or he is just playing along, when the President gets played, my country gets played. Senator Bob Menendez made a comment of the leader from his own party that it seemed like his talking points were coming directly from Tehran.

When the President says and his administration says that there is an agreement and the leadership of Iran is immediately refuting the terms of that agreement, in any way, there is no meeting of the minds at all. Over the course of this debate, whether we go back 10 years or we go back over the course of the last 12 to 18 months, Iran has made a tactical decision that they will benefit from billions of dollars of economic benefit in return for pursuing nuclear capability, but doing it just a little bit slower than they were previously. I think we need to understand that our enemies do not respect weakness. They only respect strength.

I support increased sanction. Mr. Sherman said at the beginning of this hearing that it is important that we have a July 1st game plan. This only goes into effect if there is no deal.

I was criticized for my expression of gratitude for the Israeli prime minister accepting the invite to come address a joint Congress. Some say that having the Israeli prime minister here undercuts America's foreign policy. One colleague on the other side of the aisle said yesterday that it is a subversion. If having the Israeli prime minister come address a joint session of Congress is undercutting American policy, then there is something wrong with America's foreign policy.

I think that we need to be posturing ourselves always from positions of strength and not weakness. I believe in American exceptionalism. We are a great country. We have seen it in Iran as we have seen it in other foreign policy challenges our country faces. There is nothing to apologize for if the President sees himself with leverage going into negotiations.

And my question in some form or fashion with my colleagues before me has been asked, but I would just like you to speak to the very simple question of if Congress passes increased sanctions, does that give this President—which only go into effect if there is no deal—does that give this President more leverage or less in his talks?

Mr. EDELMAN. Congressman Zeldin, I cannot imagine how it cannot give him more leverage as the previous sanctions have already given us leverage. I agree with Ray that economic sanctions alone are not enough. I think we need to do a few other things. I spoke in my statement about the importance of convincing Iran that the military option is serious and real. The administration likes to say all options are on the table. I think when the Supreme Leader gives speeches ridiculing that behind banners that say ''America can't do a damn thing to us,'' it tells you that they are not convinced that it is real and they need to be convinced that it is real because that is part of getting them to the point that I think Mr. Hannah was talking about earlier, concluding that a diplomatic solution is the best option for them because the other options, both economic and military are worse.

Mr. HANNAH. Congressman, I think that in theory it should give you more leverage, makes it much more difficult to have more leverage when you have the leader of the negotiations, the President of the United States himself arguing against it, saying he doesn't want it and saying that such action would, in fact, constitute grounds for unraveling the international coalition and for our enemy walking away from the table and resuming its nuclear program. So I think that is extremely problematic. I think it could work, but I am worried about it.

Mr. TAKEYH. I will say that if it is the administration's position that the sanctions are unnecessary at this stage, then they are obligated to say how do they propose to change the dynamics of stalemated talks.

Mr. EINHORN. The administration says pressure is necessary at this stage. It just believes that there is sufficient pressure now augmented by the drop in the oil prices. There is sufficient pressure. The question is whether there should be what would be perceived internationally as a premature and unnecessary provocation.

Mr. ZELDIN. I thank the panel and again to the committee and to the chairman. Last night I was in my office rereading the U.S. Constitution and I see components of it talking about the power of the purse of Congress, the ratification of treaties, the declaration of war. Those out there who said that this body is not an equal branch of government and does not have a role in America's foreign policy I would recommend that it would be good reading to look at the U.S. Constitution and some of its analysis. I yield back the balance of my time.

Mr. PERRY. The gentleman yields. The gentleman from California, Mr. Lowenthal, is recognized.

Mr. LOWENTHAL. Thank you, Mr. Chair. And I want to thank the panelists for having this discussion today and educating us. It couldn't be more timely obviously at this moment, especially after the President in the State of the Union asked Congress not to impose any sanctions until the final details of the agreement come out.

So my question and I think you have all dealt with it and I first want to associate myself with many of the comments by other members, especially Mr. Cicilline, who I am very supportive of diplomacy if it works. So the question I have in a much more specific way is in the Senate there is the Kirk-Menendez Bill that has been introduced, which really talks about specific, what to do now, specifically. And I think Mr. Einhorn has already kind of answered this question, but I would like to know from Ambassador Edelman and Mr. Hannah and Mr. Takeyh, would you recommend that we take up that bill or a bill similar to that, that specific bill which really does do—increases sanctions if the interim agreement doesn't lead to a comprehensive agreement. It is real clear. Should we be dealing with that specific bill now?

Mr. EDELMAN. Mr. Lowenthal, I would, were I in your shoes, bearing in mind, the understandable concerns that Mr. Connolly and others have raised. Look, I spent 30 years as a career diplomat, so I, too, support diplomatic efforts. I don't think there is anybody on this panel or really very many people who follow this issue who don't believe that a diplomatic solution would be far preferable to having to resort to other means, particularly military. But having said that, the key, I think, is what you said. Supporting diplomacy, if it is successful. And one of the challenges of diplomacy is not losing sight of what the objective is. And I have seen unfortunately many times where negotiators, understandably having been involved for a very long time, become very committed to the success of the negotiation with less concern about exactly what the outcome is. And we need to remember what outcome I think all of us are hoping for which is that we end up with a region that does not have an Iran that has a nuclear weapons capability or on the threshold of one.

Mr. LOWENTHAL. Just before I go on to Mr. Hannah and

Mr. Takeyh, I want to follow up on your answer. You know, timing is obviously critically important and I think that is what you are really saying in part is all the timing.

Recently, Prime Minister David Cameron said it is the opinion of the United Kingdom that further sanctions or the threat of sanctions won't help at all now. And as was pointed out already by the representatives of Great Britain, France, Germany, European Union recently wrote a very powerful op ed piece saying that new sanctions now introduced could eliminate this coalition, could break the unity. Do you agree with that?

Mr. EDELMAN. It is clearly a challenge for alliance management, but I think some of that challenge has to be met by firm leadership from the United States. Secondly, I think the question is are the sanctions that are being discussed now immediate or are they prospective? Somehow the Iranians are free to announce that they are building two more nuclear facilities which couldn't be less in the spirit of these negotiations than saying if the negotiations don't reach a successful outcome, then Iran would be subject to more sanctions. Somehow that is not a provocation to us, but the Congress considering sanctions is.

I will tell you, Mr. Lowenthal, one of the reasons I don't believe the Iranians have been terribly serious about this process and bringing it to a conclusion, one of the signals to me that they are not, is the fact that they are not demanding that the administration come to the Congress for approval of whatever agreement is reached. If they were serious, and were intent on an agreement that would outlive this Presidential administration, they would say we will only agree to something that you take to the Congress so that we know it has gone some permanence to it.

Mr. LOWENTHAL. Thank you. I would like to go on to Mr. Hannah.

Mr. HANNAH. Yes, I would associate myself with Ambassador Edelman's remarks, Congressman, and just simply note that if I was sitting across the table from the Iranians, I would want the Congress as active and making as much noise and being as frustrated as possible.

Mr. LOWENTHAL. So you would be supportive of us taking up the Kirk-Menendez Bill as soon as possible?

Mr. HANNAH. I certainly would. I think any activity up here does give, should give our negotiators leverage to say this Congress is running out of patience.

Mr. LOWENTHAL. Regardless what our other members of the P5+1 are saying?

Mr. HANNAH. So long as the President of the United States is agreeing with them that this is grounds for collapsing these negotiations, if you had the United States explaining to our P5+1 what needs to happen here and what these sanctions are all about, I think you would mitigate the problem enormously.

Mr. LOWENTHAL. Mr. Takeyh?

Mr. TAKEYH. I would say, Congressman, that at this particular stage, given the differences between Congress and the President on this issue has not helped the negotiations at all and is not helping our negotiators. I would actually advise instead of the Congress, the White House to come to Congress and negotiate with it what kind of a sanctions bill they want, what kind of equities they want to negotiate. I think Bob mentioned that.

Mr. LOWENTHAL. Before the end of June they should be coming, now publicly, after they have asked us not to do sanctions?

Mr. TAKEYH. They should have come long ago saying this is what we want to see in a sanctions bill and the Legislative and the Executive Branch can work something out. They do have interlocutors on the Hill, far more ready than they do in Tehran. And in that sense, I think the unity of the two branches of government are critical for success of diplomacy.

Mr. PERRY. The gentleman's time has expired.

Mr. LOWENTHAL. Thank you.

Mr. PERRY. The Chair now recognizes Mr. Emmer from Minnesota.

Mr. EMMER. Thank you, Mr. Chair, and to the distinguished panel, thank you for your time. I just have a couple of follow ups.

For Ambassador Edelman, I think you have answered it now. At the beginning, you talked about recommending. You recommended threatening or imposing new sanctions or additional sanctions. From your most recent comments are you focused now on sanctions in the event these current negotiations are not concluded by the pending deadline?

Mr. EDELMAN. Yes, sir.

Mr. EMMER. And if you could do me one more favor and maybe I will take this to others, sanctions are only as effective, can only be effective if they are not hollow, in other words, if they have an impact. It really doesn't matter what somebody says whether they are going to honor it or not. If additional sanctions are imposed, whether now or once the deadline expires, are those sanctions going to be effective? Is that a rhetorical question?

Mr. EDELMAN. Obviously, Mr. Emmer, it will depend a little bit on what you and your colleagues consider and what you put into the bill and how it is structured. I do think that there is, although Ray has written elsewhere, that Iran is the most sanctioned country in the world, I do think that there is still room, there are other sectors of the economy that haven't been hit yet, so I think there is still room to turn up the pressure. And I think there are other things we can do and members of the panel have suggested it, Mr. Sherman for one, others have. It shouldn't be just economic pressure. I think there ought to be support for democracy movements inside Iran. I think there ought to be broadcasting. I think there is a whole panoply of things we ought to be doing to put the regime on notice that we will oppose it across the board as it seeks to exert its hegemony in the region.

Mr. EMMER. Mr. Einhorn, in the interest of time I have a different question for you. In the beginning, during your testimony, you indicated that you believe continued strong pressure, but not sanctions, additional sanctions at this point, would be the prudent course of action. But then you went on to say that we have time, that we don't need to act now and if the current deadline expires, comes and goes, that we still have time. How much time do we have, sir? What do you recommend? Another 6 months?

Mr. EINHORN. I wouldn't put any arbitrary time limit on it. All I am saying is that the current interim arrangement works to our benefit much more than it works for Iran. Their nuclear program is frozen in all meaningful respects. The sanctions are biting very hard. I think if we cannot get the deal we want to get, we can afford to wait. They are under much more pressure than we are.

Mr. EMMER. Let me ask you, sorry to interrupt, but in the interest of time, if the United States, our interest is peace and prosperity, not only in that region, but across the globe, and presumably that is one of the underlying reasons for these negotiations with this regime, what is Iran's incentive for a viable deal?

Mr. EINHORN. Their main incentive is to get out from under the sanctions that are crippling their economy. I think that is what brought them to the table. That is their incentive.

Mr. EMMER. But sir, and again, we get limited with time, we have already heard testimony that their policy has not changed. Their goal remains the same and that is the elimination of Israel and the United States. So getting out from underneath sanctions, again, I am going to ask you, what is their incentive then is just to bypass any real solution so that they can accomplish their goal?

Mr. EINHORN. A number of panelists have made this point. They have to have a clear choice. They have to realize that they can't achieve their goal except by agreeing to a deal that meets our requirements.

Mr. EMMER. Well then, let me ask Dr. Takeyh. Isn't the only way that you can give them a clear choice is if you have some choice? In other words, you either reach an agreement and eliminate the nuclear prospect or these sanctions will be imposed?

Mr. TAKEYH. I think at this particular stage, even in the aftermath of an agreement, Iran will maintain a nuclear infrastructure of some capability and after expiration of a period of time, perhaps a decade or so, then is free to move toward industrialization of that capability. So we will have to live with or without an agreement with an Iran with a sizeable nuclear infrastructure.

Mr. EMMER. Thank you. I yield back.

Mr. PERRY. Chair thanks the gentleman and the Chair recognizes the gentleman from Florida, Mr. Clawson.

Mr. CLAWSON. Thanks for hanging in there y'all. I think this is just about it. Israeli leaders have repeatedly indicated that they are prepared to take military action against Iranian nuclear facilities. They have also stated that they will not feel constrained from such action even if the P5+1 signs a deal with Tehran that leaves its uranium enrichment program intact. And there we have in our office what we call the Tel Aviv conundrum. The administration cuts a deal with Tehran. The Israelis feel even more vulnerable and even more unprotected.

I guess my question is how do you all view that? What would the Obama administration do and how should we think about that? Israel's defense and safety is of very big importance to me and my constituents and it feels like this train is just going down the track and our friends are going to be left by the wayside. Am I seeing something incorrect here or how would you all respond?

Mr. EDELMAN. Mr. Clawson, let me make just a couple of points in response to what you said. Number one, I do think that Israeli potential, Israeli action is a major concern for Tehran and I will give you some evidence for that. You may recall a couple of years back, Prime Minister Netanyahu made a speech at the U.N. General Assembly where he had the cartoon with the sort of Wile E. Coyote bomb and had the marker for how much 20 percent low-enriched uranium Iran would have to get before he would feel constrained to do something. And what was interesting is between that period and then the negotiation between the Joint Plan of Action and the Iranians very, very carefully kept below that level. They were down blending even then, even before the Joint Plan of Action, some of their 20 percent low enriched uranium.

That suggests to me that at least somebody's red line had some—held some concern for the Iranian leadership. Point number one.

Two, I said in my statement that I think the United States ought to be talking with Israel now about what kinds of capabilities Israel thinks it needs to deal with this problem, in part, because I think that is an incentive for Iran to reach a deal. I think just the process of beginning those discussions with Israel could begin to have some impact on Tehran's calculus about this.

And then the final point I would make is I think it was, I am not sure who it was in the administration who gave an interview with The Atlantic with Jeff Goldberg, thank you, suggesting that the administration had blocked Israel from taking any action on this, but I think it was very, very ill considered both because of the manner in which it treated an ally, but also because it undercut the potential impact that Israeli calculations might have on Tehran.

Mr. CLAWSON. So are you implying that Israel is a more effective deterrent to Tehran than we are, given the approach of our current administration?

Mr. EDELMAN. Mr. Clawson, deterrence is always a function of capability and will. And I think in this case, I think right now Israel might not, well, they don't have as much capability as the United States does to inflict military damage on Iran's program, but——

Mr. CLAWSON. But they have more will.

Mr. EDELMAN. But they probably are perceived to have more will.

Mr. HANNAH. Yes, Congressman, I would just say I agree with Ambassador Edelman that it is unbelievably unfortunate that the United States has actually been talking down the Israeli military option, the way they have, because I think the credibility of an Israeli strike is something that has been or should be quite useful and helpful to the United States.

Having said all of that, I think if we get to the kind of agreement that we are headed to with only a 12-month margin in which the Iranians could race to a bomb, if we sign on to that, if the international community does, I think it will put an Israeli military option at great jeopardy. It will put Israel in an unbelievably difficult position. And I would hope that the United States, as part of any agreement, would come to the Israelis and provide some very concrete, specific assurances on what action we will take, including military action at the first indication we have of an Iranian material violation of any agreement going forward. I think that kind of agreement with the Israelis is going to be essential if we are not going to force the Israelis to either go it alone or swallow an agreement that leaves them 7 minutes away from an Iranian ballistic missile with a warhead on it.

Mr. CLAWSON. So what I am hearing from all of you, at least the two that have spoken, is that our current approach is disjointed, not just from Congress, but moreover from our biggest friends in the region.

Mr. HANNAH. I would agree.

Mr. CLAWSON. Yield back.

Mr. PERRY. The gentleman yields. Gentlemen, you are at the finish line, however, you have got me standing in the way, you and lunch, so I will try and be brief here. I do find it somewhat fascinating that the conversations, some of them, center around the fact that if we impose or have this discussion about the imposition of more sanctions or the panoply of other measures, as the Ambassador says it, that somehow we are the ones that are scuttling the negotiations. I find that fascinating in the context of these folks, the Iranians in particular, that have obfuscated, have been historical obfuscators and strategic delayers of unparalleled proportion. And I think the world can see that over the course of time, they have marched forward, maybe in fits and starts at some point, but have marched forward with their program and the rest of the world has found a way over time to forgive more and more and more of it and this is just a continuation of that.

So with that though, I am just curious, the IAEA has uncovered significant evidence that Iran has engaged in activities related to the development of nuclear explosive devices or warheads and it refers to such activities as possible military dimensions or PMD.

Ambassador, can you tell us were these issues mentioned in the interim agreement, the PMD issues?

Mr. EDELMAN. In the Joint Plan of Action, the issues of PMD are left to the IAEA to adjudicate with Iran and so far the IAEA has not been able to make very much progress on that. And in some areas, like the military explosive activity that may have taken place at the Parchin facility, it seems pretty clear from IAEA reports that the Iranians are very far along in cleansing and cleaning up that site, so it won't be possible to really learn much from going there.

Mr. PERRY. So we are leaving it up to the IAEA, but wouldn't you agree that that the PMD, the military dimension, if Iran were seeking purely a civilian power generation kind of approach to this whole thing, I don't think a whole lot of the world would have as much difficulty as we have right now. It is the military dimension.

What is in the United States' or the West's interest and the coalition partners' interest to allow the IAEA to negotiate that portion of the agreement?

Mr. EDELMAN. Well, the IAEA certainly has a lot of technical expertise that can help them get to the bottom of this, but I agree, I think, with the thrust of your question as I said earlier, it is inconceivable to me that we can design a monitoring and verification regime for any agreement without having satisfied ourselves that we understand the past military dimensions of Iranian activity. I don't know how you would even know where to look if you hadn't gotten to the bottom of most of these issues, if not all of them.

Mr. PERRY. It seems to me that regarding the military dimension certainly we want the IAEA's technical expertise, but we must set the course and the foundation and the vision for what will be allowed and what will not be allowed, and if we leave that lock, stock, and barrel to them, who knows where we might end up. It sounds incredibly irresponsible to me which goes to the other point where some folks say well, the President should be coming to the Congress to discuss what is next and what sanctions may be. I don't know if you have watched current events, if you are aware, but he has just said you folks stay out of it, I will handle it. So we are duty bound by our duty to the country and to our constituents to do something in the face of what we see as irresponsibility.

With that, a key component is the delivery system, the delivery capability. Shouldn't the long-term agreement include limitations on the ballistic missile capability?

Go ahead, Mr. Ambassador?

Mr. EDELMAN. Well, I certainly agree with that. I think it is a fact that no country in the world has had a ballistic missile program of the scale and scope of Iran's without actually moving forward to develop a nuclear weapon.

Mr. PERRY. Mr. Hannah, should we be concerned? I just saw recent reports. I am sure you saw the photographs of the tower of the alleged ballistic missile located within. Should we, as Americans, be concerned? Is this something expected, unexpected?

Mr. HANNAH. I think we absolutely should be concerned, Congressman. There is absolutely no purpose for Iran to have an intercontinental ballistic missile system capable of hitting the United States and Western Europe unless it is married to a nuclear warhead. There is no military rationale for it.

Mr. PERRY. I mean this may seem elementary, but what purpose does the ballistic missile system have regarding a nuclear warhead in a peaceful nuclear program? Where is the nexus? What am I missing? What are the American people—what are all of us fools missing that think that we ought to impose the panoply on Iran? What are we missing? Am I missing something, Mr. Hannah?

Mr. HANNAH. I don't think so, Congressman, other than the fact that the Iranians have insisted this is a red line for them. They will not discuss it and if we want a deal on the nuclear issues, then we need to leave this issue of ballistic missiles out of the negotiations. That is all I am aware of.

Mr. PERRY. It is nice to know they are in the driver's seat. With that, I will yield back. Sorry, I thought you were free, but Mr. Issa is here, so I recognize the gentleman from California.

Mr. ISSA. Thank you. You are almost free. I want to try to put something in perspective and then ask a very broad question. I think when you are the last to ask a wrap-up question sometimes has less fact and more history.

A silver-haired gentleman over my shoulder, the late Henry Hyde, he hadn't served 5 years in this body, even though he served 35 years, when Iran, under its present government using the guise of ''students,'' took hostage all of our Embassy personnel and kept them for 1,000 days. Negotiating with the Jimmy Carter administration as though there was something to negotiate, but never providing them until it was in their best interest. Mr. Hyde was still a junior member, a lot less gray hair, as they proceeded to fund terrorism around the world including blowing up our Marines in '82 in Beirut, including the formation funding of Hezbollah from its inception until today.

Hafez Assad was still running Syria and counted on Iran to provide him with money and munitions for decades between the time Henry Hyde was a fairly young man and now approaching his 100th birthday. We have gone 35 years with a government that funds and exports terrorism, who has used its vast oil wealth not even to create in their country, even to create the ability to refine their own oil into gasoline. Their priorities have been on exporting terrorism, destabilizing both the Sunni Arab world and quite frankly the opportunity for peace in Israel. For 35 years, you can point to Iran as the single closest reason of why we do not have peace for the Palestinians and the Israelis.

So let me ask the question. I will start with Mr. Hannah, I will go to all of you. Why in the world are we negotiating and talking today about a small part of a small delay in their ambition to have the ultimate weapon to give them impunity to continue doing what they have been doing for 35 years?

Mr. HANNAH. If that is the objective, and if that is where we are headed, as I have said in my testimony, Congressman, I don't think it is worth a candle to be going down that route, especially if we are ignoring the fact that this export of terror has only escalated and accelerated in the last year. I don't think that should be the objective. I think our objective should be to present them with a choice, that either you stop this nuclear program that is the greatest threat to international security that exists today or your regime will be put at serious risk by the United States, by the combination of a threat of military force that is very credible and crippling economic sanctions that essentially shut down the Iranian economy. Without that choice, I think this is a fool's errand.

Mr. ISSA. Mr. Takeyh, obviously, the whole day we have been talking about a fairly narrow part of our relationship or lack thereof with Tehran, but again, a fundamental question. It has been asked wonderfully as to whether or not we should tag on to the back end of the President's negotiations, but the bigger question is why is a Member of Congress who is still a first lieutenant in the Army with no gray hair—not much hair actually at the time—and now 35 years later is sitting here, why is it that I should believe that we should even be talking about the scope of well, if you will just slow down to a crawl your nuclear development then we have got a deal and completely ignore the human rights violations inside Tehran, or Iran, but particularly the constant export of terrorism in which country by country, it is Iran's goal to in fact, destabilize countries, both are friends and our foes within the Arab and Muslim world?

Mr. TAKEYH. I think I agree with the thrust of your question, Congressman. We shouldn't be ignoring human rights abuses in Iran. We shouldn't be ignoring the fact that Iran has a very aggressive regional policy today, and particularly, we shouldn't be ignoring the fact that something that we don't talk about is Iran today is undertaking military invasion of Iraq with the seeming complicity of the Iraqi Government and at least the passive indifference of the international community.

Mr. ISSA. I don't mean to interrupt you, because your answers are great, but as many of us that were on the dais earlier know, Iran was providing the expertise to blow up, dismember and kill our people from the very first days we put boots on the ground in Iraq, they were providing advanced IED capability. So it is not like they haven't been doing that steadily including hundreds, perhaps thousands of Americans are dead because of their assistance, but please continue.

Mr. TAKEYH. I would just say that all activities of Iran that are unsavory of which the catalog is a long one, and the principal victims of the Iranian regime are the Iranian people. And then everybody else in the region. All those should be part of the American policy. Nuclear agreement or not, in my view, we are destined to remain adversaries with this particular regime and we should approach the relationship accordingly.

Mr. ISSA. Thank you. Mr. Einhorn.

Mr. EINHORN. Congressman, you asked the basic question, why should we be negotiating on the nuclear issue with a regime that has done all these terrible, destabilizing things. And I think the reason is that if we can stop their march toward nuclear weapons, then we can prevent a situation where they can do all of these bad things, but under the cover of a nuclear weapons capability. In other words, they could be empowered to do much worse. That is why it is important to deal with the nuclear issue. At the same time——

Mr. ISSA. Let me characterize, Chairman, if you will give me a little indulgence. If I am characterizing your statement, what you are saying in a nutshell is if they get a nuke, we will never be able to stop them from terrorizing all of their neighbors, exporting terrorism with impunity?

Mr. EINHORN. I don't mean to say that.

Mr. ISSA. Well, but you are saying is we can stop them, they won't be able to do it. For 35 years, they have never quit doing it. So if they get a nuke, not only will they not quit doing it, but we won't be able to encourage them to quit doing it. Is that correct?

Mr. EINHORN. I think with a nuke, they will be empowered to do worse. It doesn't mean that if we get a nuclear agreement they are going to stop doing that. We are going to have to counter them on these other behaviors with or without a nuclear agreement and we should be doing more of that as some of the other panelists have mentioned.

Mr. ISSA. Ambassador, you look like you have got your mic on?

Mr. EDELMAN. Yes, Congressman Issa, your question cuts very close to the bone for me. When I was a junior foreign service officer and was special assistant to George Schultz, I was the person who had to wake him up in the middle of the night when the Marine barracks was bombed in Beirut. I went to Beirut with him in April 1983 after our Embassy was blown up and Bob Ames, the national intelligence officer for Middle East was killed. I served as Under Secretary for Defense for Policy for 4 years in the Bush administration from 2005 to 2009. And had to watch as the Sheibani Network and others, as you indicated, were killing American men and women in Iraq. I had to watch after I made six trips to Lebanon to help arm the Lebanese armed forces to try and create an independent military to withstand—to stand the country up after Syrian forces had withdrawn after the assassination of Rafik Hariri and watched Iran's terrorist proxies in Lebanon, upend all of that in May 2008.

So I feel the gravamen of your question to my core. And as I suggested in my statement, we have to be prepared to contest Iran in its struggle to dominate the region across the board on all dimensions. I do think it is worth negotiating with them on the nuclear issue if we can stop them from getting a nuclear capability. I have very grave concerns, as I said earlier in the hearing, that we have retreated well beyond that red line to the point that what we may end up doing is ratifying an Iran with an industrial scale enrichment capability on the threshold of a nuclear bomb.

Mr. ISSA. Thank you. Mr. Chairman, in closing I pointed to my old friend, the late Henry Hyde. When I was a freshman of Lebanese-American descent or Lebanese descent, an American, Henry Hyde allowed me to go on a codel. And the first speech I ever made in a foreign country I made in Lebanon at our Embassy there, just above the monument, the memorial to those men and women that were killed both at the barracks and at the Embassy because our Embassy was also blown up. And at that time I said Hezbollah is a cancer on Lebanese society. What I wish I could go back and say in that speech is something a little fuller. Hezbollah is a cancer on Lebanese society funded, supported, paid for by Iran and until we stop Iran from exporting terrorism, there will not be free people in Iran, in Syria, in Lebanon, and I fear in most of the Arab and Muslim world.

So Mr. Chairman, thank you so much for this hearing today. It is a good start on pushing back against giving up something that is as worth fighting for as the Cold War was for most of my parents' lives. Thank you. I yield back.

Mr. PERRY. The gentleman yields. The Chair thanks the gentlemen for their testimony and their service today and also the participants in the hearing and with that, this hearing is adjourned.

[Whereupon, at 12:49 p.m., the committee was adjourned.]

APPENDIX

FULL COMMITTEE HEARING NOTICE
COMMITTEE ON FOREIGN AFFAIRS
U.S. HOUSE OF REPRESENTATIVES
WASHINGTON, DC 20515-6128

Edward R. Royce (R-CA), Chairman

January 20, 2015

TO: MEMBERS OF THE COMMITTEE ON FOREIGN AFFAIRS

You are respectfully requested to attend an OPEN hearing of the Committee on Foreign Affairs, to be held in Room 2172 of the Rayburn House Office Building (and available live on the Committee website at http://www.ForeignAffairs.house.gov):

DATE: Tuesday, January 27, 2015

TIME: 10:00 a.m.

SUBJECT: Iran Nuclear Negotiations After the Second Extension: Where Are They Going?

WITNESSES: The Honorable Eric S. Edelman
                 Distinguished Fellow
                 Center for Strategic and Budgetary Assessments

                 Mr. John Hannah
                 Senior Fellow
                 Foundation for Defense of Democracies

                 Ray Takeyh, Ph.D.
                 Senior Fellow for Middle Eastern Studies
                 Council on Foreign Relations

                 The Honorable Robert Einhorn
                 Senior Fellow
                 Foreign Policy Program
                 The Brookings Institution

By Direction of the Chairman

The Committee on Foreign Affairs seeks to make its facilities accessible to persons with disabilities. If you are in need of special accommodations, please call 202/225-5021 at least four business days in advance of the event, whenever practicable. Questions with regard to special accommodations in general (including availability of Committee materials in alternative formats and assistive listening devices) may be directed to the Committee.

COMMITTEE ON FOREIGN AFFAIRS
MINUTES OF FULL COMMITTEE HEARING

Day __Tuesday__ Date ___01/27/15___ Room ___2172___

Starting Time __10:07 a.m.__ Ending Time __12:49 p.m.__

Recesses __0__ (____ to ____) (____ to ____) (____ to ____) (____ to ____) (____ to ____) (____ to ____)

Presiding Member(s)

Edward R. Royce, Chairman,
Rep. Ileana Ros-Lehtinen, Rep. Ted Poe, Rep. Scott Perry

Check all of the following that apply:

Open Session ☑   Electronically Recorded (taped) ☑
Executive (closed) Session ☐   Stenographic Record ☑
Televised ☑

TITLE OF HEARING:

Iran Nuclear Negotiations After the Second Extension: Where Are They Going?

COMMITTEE MEMBERS PRESENT:

See Attached Sheet.

NON-COMMITTEE MEMBERS PRESENT:

None.

HEARING WITNESSES: Same as meeting notice attached? Yes ☑ No ☐
(If "no", please list below and include title, agency, department, or organization.)

STATEMENTS FOR THE RECORD: *(List any statements submitted for the record.)*

SFR - Rep. Gerald Connolly

TIME SCHEDULED TO RECONVENE _____
or
TIME ADJOURNED __12:49 p.m.__

Jean Marter, Director of Committee Operations

HOUSE COMMITTEE ON FOREIGN AFFAIRS
FULL COMMITTEE HEARING

PRESENT	MEMBER
X	Edward R. Royce, CA
X	Christopher H. Smith, NJ
X	Ileana Ros-Lehtinen, FL
	Dana Rohrabacher, CA
X	Steve Chabot, OH
X	Joe Wilson, SC
	Michael T. McCaul, TX
X	Ted Poe, TX
X	Matt Salmon, AZ
X	Darrell Issa, CA
	Tom Marino, PA
X	Jeff Duncan, SC
X	Mo Brooks, AL
X	Paul Cook, CA
X	Randy Weber, TX
X	Scott Perry, PA
X	Ron DeSantis, FL
X	Mark Meadows, NC
X	Ted Yoho, FL
X	Curt Clawson, FL
	Scott, DesJarlais, TN
	Reid Ribble, WI
X	Dave Trott, MI
X	Lee Zeldin, NY
X	Tom Emmer, MN

PRESENT	MEMBER
	Eliot L. Engel, NY
X	Brad Sherman, CA
	Gregory W. Meeks, NY
	Albio Sires, NJ
X	Gerald E. Connolly, VA
X	Theodore E. Deutch, FL
	Brian Higgins, NY
	Karen Bass, CA
X	William Keating, MA
X	David Cicilline, RI
	Alan Grayson, FL
	Ami Bera, CA
X	Alan S. Lowenthal, CA
	Grace Meng, NY
X	Lois Frankel, FL
X	Tulsi Gabbard, HI
X	Joaquin Castro, TX
X	Robin Kelly, IL
X	Brendan Boyle, PA

MATERIAL SUBMITTED FOR THE RECORD BY THE HONORABLE EDWARD R. ROYCE, A REPRESENTATIVE IN CONGRESS FROM THE STATE OF CALIFORNIA, AND CHAIRMAN, COMMITTEE ON FOREIGN AFFAIRS

January 26, 2015

Chairman Ed Royce
Committee on Foreign Affairs
U.S. House of Representatives

Dear Chairman Royce:

As you meet Tuesday to discuss possible sanctions against Iran, we would like to introduce you to Amir Hekmati. Amir was born in Arizona and raised in Michigan. He is a decorated combat veteran, serving in the Marines in Iraq during a time of war. He is an uncle, a brother, and a son. He is also an American being imprisoned in Iran.

For over three years, Amir has languished behind the walls of Iran's Evin prison. During this time, he has been tortured, abused, and mistreated while the threat of a death sentence has hung over his head. Amir's health has deteriorated, he is chronically ill, and the conditions of his imprisonment keep Amir weak and malnourished. While he faces real threats to his safety and security as a prisoner in Evin, his father fights a different battle—not only for Amir's freedom, but for his own life.

Ali Hekmati, Amir's father, has terminal brain cancer. He has recently suffered several strokes that have forced him to leave his job as a microbiology professor. He now requires around-the-clock care. The need for Amir to be released and returned home to help his family grows more each day.

We appreciate that your job is a difficult one. We simply ask that, during Tuesday's hearing, do not forget our son. Amir is a man of character, innocent of the charges brought against him, and held hostage to politics.

For three years, he has been away from the family he loves and the country he has served. It is long past time for a bipartisan effort to be made on Amir's behalf to free him and bring him home.

Respectfully,

The Hekmati Family

Statement for the Record
Submitted by Mr. Connolly of Virginia

It has been over 1 year since the Joint Plan of Action (JPOA) went into effect. Negotiators have extended the talks beyond the original timeframe and pressure is mounting for results. In the pursuit of this historic opportunity, we must be certain that the Iranians are negotiating in good faith. We cannot accept the status quo under the guise of additional extensions in perpetuity. With each extension, the argument that additional pressure must be applied to Iran becomes more salient.

The JPOA framework does arrest the Iran nuclear program, and the value of the interim agreement as our best available option for preventing Iran from obtaining a nuclear weapon should not be understated. The Administration's offer to cooperate with Congress to implement immediate and additional sanctions should Iran back away from the negotiating table or fail to uphold its obligations is welcome.

The P5+1 negotiations constitute a multilateral effort to engage the Islamic Republic on an issue of profound import to the region. The talks are the first meaningful engagement the U.S. has had with Iran in decades and there remains a profound lack of trust on both sides. Consequently, the cornerstone of the talks and any ultimate agreement must be verification, transparency, and compliance. It is worth noting in this respect that the International Atomic Energy Agency (IAEA) has consistently reported that Iran has complied with all JPOA obligations.

Further, the JPOA has measured significant progress on its effort to halt Iran's march towards a nuclear weapon. Before the JPOA went into effect, Iran was enriching uranium stockpiles, constructing a heavy water reactor at Arak, readying 9,000 additional centrifuges for operation, and allowing inspectors only sporadic access to nuclear facilities. Under the JPOA, Iran has eliminated all 20 percent enriched uranium, suspended all enrichment above 5 percent, stopped construction at Arak, kept 9,000 centrifuges offline, and provided inspectors with daily access to its nuclear facilities. Further, our domestic embargo and financial, banking, petroleum, trade, terrorism, and human rights sanctions remain in place under the JPOA.

This Committee has heard testimony on the alternatives to negotiations with Iran. At a November hearing before the Subcommittee on the Middle East and North Africa, General Michael Hayden stated that the euphemistically termed "kinetic" option would actually accelerate Iran's pursuit and development of a nuclear weapon. It would also deprive us of one of the most valuable components of the JPOA which is enhanced surveillance of Iran's nuclear program.

JPOA progress notwithstanding, the Administration must understand that support for continued negotiations in Congress is far from unconditional. We must see progress towards a broad outline of an agreement before the self-imposed, informal deadline of March 1. Similarly, Congressional patience will be severely diminished if not completely exhausted should we reach the June 30 deadline without a final agreement. The ultimate question about an extension is: are we progressing to a verifiable and enforceable nuclear termination agreement or is Iran just playing for time?

It is Iran's own actions that have isolated the Islamic Republic from the rest of the world. Human rights abuses, provocative intervention into regional conflicts, and an illicit nuclear program have necessitated the construction of a broad and effective sanctions regime. The P5+1 have placed on the table an alternative to Iran's current destructive trajectory. That alternative is the prospect of a high-quality final agreement in which Iran must answer difficult questions regarding outstanding items such as IAEA monitoring, the peaceful purposes of the Fordow enrichment facility, and centrifuge research and development. Congress has thus far been a constructive partner in the pursuit of a final deal, but our patience is wearing thin.

[NOTE: Material submitted for the record by Mr. John Hannah, senior fellow, Foundation for Defense of Democracies, entitled "The Case for Deadline-Triggered Sanctions on Iran," is not reprinted here but is available in committee records or may be accessed via the Internet at http://docs.house.gov/meetings/FA/FA00/20150127/102846/HHRG-114-FA00-Wstate-HannahJ-20150127-SD001.pdf]